For m
who d'
to tell. Love you all,
Ella

Aloisia's New Beginnings & Other Stories

Ella Benndorf

Also by Ella Benndorf:

RECIPE COLLECTION
Mom's Soup for You

Available on Amazon:

BIOGRAPHY
Walter Benndorf, The Moulding of a German-
Canadian

BIOGRAPHY
Aloisia: The Making of a Frontier Woman

Aloisia's
New Beginnings
& Other Stories

Ella Benndorf

WhatWorks Media

Vancouver, Canada

Cover Painting: Ella Benndorf

Cover design & Layout: Michele Hall

Editing: Michele Hall

Throughout this book, we have used the
symbol of the oak which represents patience,
courage, strength and survival, wisdom and
dignity. These are the very traits that the author
feels embody her parents, Aloisia and Franz,
who worked hard as pioneers and farmers
in the new frontier of British Columbia.

ISBN-13: 978-1984005557

WhatWorks Media
Vancouver, Canada

Contents

Aloisia's New Beginnings

Aloisia Schropp and Franz Baumgartner were both born in 1896 and grew up on their family's respective farms in Southern Germany. Though they had to work hard, they always had enough to eat; nobody went without the essentials. In fact, during their youth Germany was considered the most socially advanced country in the western world.

When World War I broke out German ports were blockaded; staples became impossible to obtain. In 1916 the German government sponsored beekeeping courses so farmers would refresh the skills required to produce honey, the most popular sugar substitute. It was at such a course that Aloisia and Franz met. Aloisia attended so she could take over beekeeping from her aging father. Franz had previously attended agricultural college but was on leave from the navy while his ship was being refitted and he wanted to study beekeeping, as this subject had not been included in the college curriculum.

After the course was completed, the two corresponded for ten years while Franz was serving in the navy, pioneering in Argentina and then back working on his family's farm again. What each considered a platonic friendship finally developed into love. They wanted to marry but the financial situation made it impossible. The Treaty of Versailles had plunged Germany into a depression: the reparations had no end in sight. To make the situation even more difficult, Aloisia was the youngest of a large family and Franz had given up his right of primogeniture due to his father's insistence on using antiquated farming techniques. Aloisia and Franz discussed immigrating to Canada and starting a new life.

The Schropp family was alarmed. Franz and Aloisia were summoned to a meeting. At the gathering the two of them pleaded for understanding—after all they were almost thirty years old.

But the family ridiculed Aloisia for even thinking of marrying Franz. Though Franz was handsome and dignified in bearing several points were against him. He was neither from her home village nor one nearby. What was he doing hundreds of kilometers from his home? Couldn't he find a wife in his own valley? Shouldn't he be helping on his farm rather than travelling around? How could this man have the nerve to imagine that Aloisia should emigrate with him to Canada? Baumgartner (that's how he was always referred to) had given up the rights of primogeniture, the excuse being that he had learned some ideas at agricultural college of which his father didn't approve. And hadn't he already traveled to Argentina? Why did he come back? Franz explained that his father had asked him to return promising to allow cleaner, more scientific methods of agriculture and had broken his promise when Franz returned. The assembled relatives found the argument weak and even irrelevant. Why

9

should Aloisia leave her comfortable two-storey brick home in a civilized country for an uncertain future? Stories were related about emigrants who left Germany with high hopes and were sorely disappointed—or were never heard of again. And if Aloisia thought she would get help of any kind of financial assistance for this marriage she was badly mistaken. They all had their own worries.

Though some of these arguments may have had a thread of validity, Aloisia suspected the real reason. Her eldest brother, Peter, wanted her to continue working on the farm in exchange for the use of a two storey brick home and food from the farm. The other relatives in the city would find it more difficult to get produce from the farm without Aloisia's watchful arrangements. All of her family, being older, knew that marriage was not always an easy road. Aloisia had more than most women her age. She should consider herself lucky. Taking everything into consideration, there was no need for her to marry anyone.

Aloisia was finally persuaded to bow to her family's pressure and Franz returned home to make immigration arrangements to Canada, alone. In May 1926, Franz was just leaving his parents' farm for the last time as an express letter arrived. It was from Aloisia. Despite her family's opposition, she wanted to join him in Canada. She could be there as early as November if he could just send an address.

While on route to board the Canadian Pacific Ship, *Minnedosa,* at Hamburg Franz replied to Aloisia's express letter. He no longer felt in the position to dare promise Aloisia anything, especially after the confrontation with her family. He did not know what situation he would find himself in or where he would finally settle. If she wanted to get her money together however, she could come to see how things were in Canada for herself. If she didn't like it, she could always return to Germany. She shouldn't rush her decision. He only knew that the Treaty of Versailles and the subsequent runaway inflation had left Germany's future hopeless.

Franz's first destination (as that of many male immigrants arriving in Canada) was the Canadian prairies where he helped with the grain harvest. He worked on a farm in Windthorst, just south of Grenfell, Saskatchewan. After three months, Franz wrote Aloisia again. He had evaluated the situation in Canada and saw much more opportunity than in Germany. He was impressed that in her last letter she said how she would love him even in poor circumstances. If Aloisia wanted to join him, she should come. Maybe she could even be in Canada by November as she had written in her last letter?

Grasshoppers were a real plague on the prairies that year. Franz had no intention of being around for the next harvest. He answered an ad in the Winnipeg Free Press looking for hired help on a mixed farming operation near Nelson, British Columbia. The ad was placed by a man called Mackereth. The location of his homestead was Broadwater on the widest part of the Columbia River. He and his family were the only inhabitants for miles around. Broadwater could only be reached by stern wheeler.

When Franz arrived he was given jobs working on all aspects of Mackereth's mixed farming operation, such as looking after a few cows and sheep. Mackereth's main objective, however was to build up a fruit ranch consisting of apples, pears, cherries, black currants, gooseberries and strawberries. To increase pollination he also kept bees. The produce had to be carried down to the Broadwater wharf from where it was loaded on the stern wheeler. When winter approached, Mackereth asked Franz to stay on to help log cedar trees and cut them into telephone pole lengths.

Franz accepted the offer and added more money to his savings; he could start thinking of buying his own place. He liked the small settlement of Renata across the lake from Broadwater as he had met some German-speaking immigrants there. But then he heard about a hunting shack on a thirty-three acre parcel of land that was for sale just a quarter of a mile up the mountain from the Mackereth property. The owner had once prospected for gold and silver and wanted to try his luck again. Franz decided to purchase the property. The prospector's dog, Trix, which could stand on his hind legs with a tobacco pipe between his teeth and then turn around, could not be taken along and would be included in the deal.

Franz had witnessed farmers living on just such rugged terrain in Switzerland (in 1923 he had fled there from Munich after some of Hitler's gang made it clear they did not appreciate his heckling) and it seemed that the Mackereths were managing. He could build up his own homestead while earning some money and free food by working for them. But whereas homes in the Swiss Alps were connected to other farms and villages by roads, Franz's acreage was completely isolated and there were, except the Mackereths, no neighbours for miles around.

As soon as Franz received Aloisia's letter that she was coming, he made some improvements to the shack. He hoisted up the roof on one side by adding five more poles (they could not be called logs by any stretch of the imagination), horizontally across the top of one wall. By this addition one foot of headroom was gained on that side—and the roof was less likely to leak.

The same day that Aloisia arrived at the Nelson train station she and Franz made their wedding vows at the local Roman Catholic Church. Two days later when Aloisia disembarked at the isolated Broadwater wharf she was bewildered when Franz led her up the steep mountainside. And when she saw the shack she was dismayed. The furniture consisted of a knee-high stove, a primitive hutch made from shipping crates (which also served as a table), two chairs and a bed. Water had to be carried in pails from a small stream along a mountain path. She saw and heard animals that were completely foreign to her: bears, cougars, wolves and coyotes. Their strange sounds pierced the surrounding wilderness both night and day.

Franz and Aloisia made some improvements. They made access to the dwelling easier by moving the door to the upper side of the slope so stairs were no longer needed. In its place they inserted a tiny window. They placed logs around the crawl space to block the wind from whistling under the floorboards. Inside, they built a partition to hide the bed.

They built a barn, smokehouse and root house. They tried planting a vegetable garden and a bit of alfalfa but the ground consisted of more rocks than earth. The deer and elk ate almost everything they planted. Cougars stalked the deer and elk. Franz cultivated a small area for propagating fruit trees, mostly from seed, and built a tall cedar fence around it for protection. He started laying an iron pipe from the stream so they wouldn't have to go so far for water. Regardless of the improvements, however, their shack was still a shack around which wolves, known only to Aloisia from fables and fairy tales, howled each night.

One day a priest was sent by the Catholic diocese in Nelson to find their homestead. He came to hear their confessions and give them Holy Communion. With some white linen and a crucifix the primitive hutch was temporarily transformed into an altar.

After the Mass Aloisia served the priest a meal including bread she had baked in the tiny cast iron stove. Franz explained (his English was much better than Aloisia's) that they had wanted to dairy farm here in Canada as they had done on their farms in Germany. The priest explained that though there were some benches of fertile soil where farming could take place and fruit trees could grow, their property, like most of the other land in the area, was mostly rocks. At least that is what he had observed hiking up to their place to find them. This was no place for farming.

He described the beautiful Fraser Valley to the west with its flat land and fertile soil. It was almost surrounded by mountains but right in the middle of the widest part was the bustling town of Chilliwack with about two thousand inhabitants. There were roads leading to dairy farms all around the valley and neighbours who

16

could give a helping hand when needed; they would not be isolated as in Broadwater. The weather was milder, much like what they must have had in Germany, the winters not being so long or harsh.

Franz and Aloisia had already realized that their land was not suitable for agriculture; the ground was more likely to break the plough than the reverse. Aloisia had used all her savings to pay for her trip and Franz had used his savings to buy the homestead. It seemed that Franz had made a terrible mistake, using all his hard-earned money to buy an isolated shack on a mountainside.

Fortunately, both realized that there was another opportunity. The entire thirty-three acres was covered with mature cedar trees. Could they not earn money by logging telephone poles? Mackereth did this to subsidize his income from his orchard. Could Franz and Aloisia log for their main source of income and forget farming at this location? This is what they decided to do, continuing to get milk and fruit from the Mackereths in exchange for their work.

Franz heard that someone had a workhorse for sale at Deer Park. It was suitable for logging.

He took the stern wheeler there, made a deal and rode the horse back on the ten mile Indian trail through the forest that wound behind Bluebird Mountain to Broadwater.

They used a washtub to carry Louise, their first-born child, into the forest with them while they worked. They skidded the logs down the mountain right past their dwelling to the river and sold them to the BC Telephone Company. The cedars were so tall and straight that they could often make three poles of various required lengths from one tree. In a little less than two years they managed to save one thousand dollars. In those days such a sum was a fortune, enough to move to the much talked about Fraser Valley without selling their thirty-three acres—which nobody would buy anyway as it had neither direct access to a road nor water.

Aloisia packed her belongings together but most of them were still in trunks as there had been no use for the finer things of life such as embroidered tablecloths and porcelain cups in their shack. She had only needed her work clothes, cast iron meat grinder, cooking utensils and bed linen. They transported the combination shelf table down to the ferry on their two-wheeled cart. Though it was rough piece of furniture (actually two pieces set on top of each other), it had once been used as an altar and had special significance to them. And of course, Aloisia's Excella sewing machine had to be crated again.

When they had their belongings assembled on the Broadwater pier they were relieved. The two year Broadwater experience had been a financial success but emotionally and physically devastating.

Just a few days after her arrival she was asked to demonstrate to the Mackereths how she could hold a frame of honeybees with her bare hands. One of them even took a picture documenting this feat. But then some bees got tangled in her wool stockings. They got alarmed (perhaps they thought the wool was a bear) and stung her all over.

Soon after that embarrassing episode she tripped on a tree root straining her ligaments. Aloisia, thirsty and unable to move, lay in the hot afternoon sun until Franz found her and carried her inside. Already pregnant with Louise, she thought she would miscarry.

Once a tree they were felling twisted in mid air, crashing down just a few feet away from baby Louise. Then there was the attack of the mother bear trying to protect her cub. Rats and mice were always around scavenging for food....

They almost starved to death the first winter of 1927/28. Fortunately, a hunter came across their homestead and shot a deer for them. After that there was venison stew, venison hamburger, venison everything until Aloisia soon felt like vomiting at the very sight of venison, let alone the smell and taste. The Mackereths gave them the head of a cow once and that was some relief.

In winter, despite a fire blazing in the little stove, the walls were often frozen. In summer it was like an oven, heating up as Aloisia often said in later years, "like a cardboard box placed in the sun."

The stern wheeler's crew dropped off mail at the Broadwater pier but that only happened twice a week. And it was a rugged mile down to the dock, and worse coming back up. Anyway, they had no money to spare for postage.

The only good that happened was the birth of Louise in the Nelson hospital and the thousand dollars in their pocket. Of course they were thankful they had survived. But Broadwater was no place to have a second child; Aloisia was expecting again.

They disembarked at Nelson and then boarded

a westward bound Canadian Pacific train. They passed through the Coast Range Mountains and got off in the small town of Agassiz at the edge of the Fraser Valley. Once there, a livery service supplied transportation down to the Fraser River where a small ferry took Aloisia, Franz and baby Louise across to Chilliwack Landing. From that pier the horse and wagon went to Chilliwack's hub, the Five Corners and pulled up at the Hart Block, the main building of which was the Hart Hotel. The Powels, who were the caretakers, helped them settle into a room and put them in contact with a helpful realtor called Hurndel.

He soon found them a fifteen acre farm in a small community a few miles west of Chilliwack called Achlitz. It was on Lickman Road just off Yale Road West, the main road going to Vancouver (later to become a section of the Trans Canada Highway). A railroad passed right behind the two-storey implement shed and there was a small barn. The land was level. Water could be hauled from a creek across the railroad track. The realtor pointed out that they could ride by democrat into Chilliwack to attend St. Mary's Church every Sunday. Aloisia could once again offer her rich alto voice to the church choir as she had in her village church in Germany. And it was only a short walk to their mailbox on Yale Road where mail was picked up and delivered every day of the week except Sunday.

The previous owner had used a converted chicken house as a dwelling. Franz and Aloisia made repairs and built partitions to create a family kitchen and two small bedrooms, one for themselves and the other for their two children, Louise and Frankie. The son had been born shortly after their arrival. They painted the interior with calcimine-tinted powder blue. Aloisia sewed some lace material she had brought from Germany into curtains. A neighbour, Nellie Kickbush, brought over a hand made red and white quilt for the Louise's and Frankie's bed. The structure was thus transformed into a cozy cottage. They even had a devoted black and white sheep dog named Rex who took the place of their dog Trix who had been left behind with the Mackereths.

The soil in Achlitz was heavy clay but with repeated applications of manure it soon became lighter and more fertile. Only in the uncultivated areas around the barn did it remain slippery in the rain. Deep, irregular cracks formed in summer. Eventually the digging of a well and water pump in the implement shed made barn and household chores much easier.

The first priority was building up a herd of dairy cows—there was money to be made with milk. It wasn't long before they were shipping as many as three cans of milk every morning, depending on the season. Each can weighed one hundred pounds whcn full, a demonstration of their agricultural acumen. They rented an adjacent fifteen acres. With more hay they could feed more livestock during the winter and thus increase their herd and milk production.

Besides milking cows (years later Aloisia used to complain that it was hard to get Franz under a cow), gardening and doing all the household chores, Aloisia looked after bees. She was continually adding supers to her hives as their numbers increased. Franz drove around the Fraser Valley selling the honey.

Then came the Fraser River flood in the spring of 1935. It was the harshest remembered in recent history. Snow had fallen more heavily that winter and in the bitter cold month of February the snow was followed by freezing rain which left a thick crust of ice over the valley fields and higher up on the surrounding foothills. Subsequent rainfalls hit the frozen layer beneath the armored earth causing massive flooding of farms. Often livestock could not lie down in their stalls because the barns were also flooded. In some cases cows and pigs sickened and died. Chickens, perched on their roosts, were more fortunate. Mice and other small field creatures faced a cold and icy death.

The high water also reached the Baumgartner farm. When the waters started to rise over the little porch and wooden floors, Franz and Aloisia suspended some furnishings in the rafters. Fortunately, Franz had replaced the ladder going to the second floor of the implement shed with a complete set of stairs (stairs he had bought at the Chilliwack auction for only one dollar). Beds and bedding, firewood and food were carried across the flooded barnyard and up to the second floor that had became their temporary home. Franz also set up a small stove, its tin smokestack jutting out of a hole cut into the side of the building. Here, the family lived for several weeks watching and waiting for the water to subside.

Because the railroad that passed by was built on a high gravel bed it was not under water, and in fact, men working on the train offered emergency supplies to adjacent farms. From the upstairs window of the implement shed, Franz shouted out his request for hip waders that would make it easier to look after the many complications caused by the high water. Finally, warm spring thaws melted the ice and the rain seeped into the soil below.

The family had survived the flood. However, the depression, "the dirty thirties", was raging. Destitute men, who had crowded into the warm cities during the winter, walked along the railroad track looking for employment, food and shelter. Peddlers and tramps tried to sell some small articles or a skill. Occasionally, Franz and Aloisia would give one of these men a meal in exchange for work around the farm. Once they heard Louise screaming and ran into the house to catch one of the men trying to molest little Louise on the kitchen table. After that incident Franz was more careful about letting strangers on their farm.

Life returned to normal again. Some may have considered them poor but it was an organized poverty. Everything was tidy. They were never without food. People passing by remarked at the neatly painted house and all the flowering fruit trees; the farm seemed to prosper despite the depression and the flood. The spreading of manure was paying off; the soil was becoming lighter, more arable. And when the hay was all up in the small loft and the grapes were harvested from their arbor, they would be a family of five. Aloisia was expecting their third child.

But life was not as idyllic as it may have seemed to a traveler passing by the little farm with its straight rows of raspberries and the flowering orchard. In reality, life was very hard and progress was only made possible by long hours of grinding toil and unrelenting frugality. All clothes were bought in thrift stores. Aloisia cut down suits and dresses to sew clothing for the children, sometimes turning the fabric inside out so the worn spots would not show. Around the farm, Frankie often wore hand-me-down clothes from Louise. Milk, meat, vegetables and fruit all came from their farm. Honey also came from their own beehives. Flour, salt and rolled oats were almost the only purchased foodstuffs. Aloisia unstitched the empty sacks, washed them and spread them out on the grass to bleach in the sun before sewing them into garments such as undershirts and aprons. One of Louise's many chores was cutting old newspapers into small pieces, the right size for toilet paper.

Pilzweger, who had helped logging telephone poles in Broadwater, and had even known Franz in Germany, had arrived and worked in exchange for board and room. Aloisia was an excellent cook and having another adult around at the table made for interesting conversation.

The spring of 1935 had been as unusually warm as the winter had been cold. The last vestiges of the great flood could only be seen at the edges of swollen sloughs that often divided farms from one another and in shallow ponds that still remained in low spots in the fields. Louise and Frankie loved to wiggle their toes in the sun-warmed, grass-lined pools.

It was June 26, the start of the summer holidays, a very happy day for Frankie because it was Louise's last day at Lickman School. Each morning he looked forward to the end of the day when his sister came up the lane again. He called her 'Idy', a name he still retained from his infancy when he could not pronounce her name properly. When school started again, he would be old enough to accompany her. In the meantime, the two would have all summer together.

And that very evening, St. Mary's Roman Catholic Church had organized a strawberry tea social. Though Franz was often away from the farm looking for bargains, "seeing how the situation was" a phrase that meant talking about politics, both locally and abroad, the rest of the family seldom had a chance to socialize. The ride into town with horse and democrat, as well as the strawberry tea, were looked forward to with great anticipation.

Franz was busy cutting the first hay-grass of the season with the horse drawn mower. Inside the house, sunshine brightening the whitewashed kitchen, Aloisia was sitting at her Excella sewing machine brought from Germany as a bride just eight years before. Rhythmic humming sounds of the foot treadle and the whirring bobbin filled the room. Frankie was playing on the floor by her side.

Suddenly there was the sound of Franz's footsteps on the porch. The screen door opened. "I had to kill Rex. I didn't even see him." Franz explained that their dog probably got excited by the rippling in the tall grass and jumped at it, not knowing that strong scissor-like blades were cutting beneath the surface. Franz heard a terrible yelping, looked over his shoulder and saw Rex covered in blood, writhing in pain. Franz stopped the horses and ran over to him. Three of Rex's legs were cut off. "I had to destroy him. I buried him beside the slough. " Aloisia nodded in agreement. What else could he do? Franz went out to the field again. It was a sunny day, perfect weather for cutting.

Aloisia fixed Frankie a bottle of milk to comfort him. She gave him his favourite toy, a bright red mechanical ladybug with feelers. It could be wound up with a key so it would hop across the floor. It had been in the parcel sent by Maria Kraus, Aloisia's cousin in Germany, the previous Christmas along with a suit for Franz. Aloisia had kept the toy hidden for Sundays and special occasions so it wouldn't wear out.

The hired man walked in. "Wouldn't Frankie like to go for a swim?" He was referring to the slough beyond their backfield that drained into Achlitz Creek. "It would take his mind off.... " He used his head to point in the direction of the field where Franz was mowing again.

Aloisia nodded but Frankie, usually so keen to go bathing with Joe, seemed reluctant. He clung to his mother's side.

"Don't you want to go, Frankie? You can play with the ladybug when you come back," she assured him.

"Do I have to go?"

"Frankie, you always like going in the water," Aloisia coaxed. She thought how clean Frankie would get; she would not have to bathe him for the strawberry tea. And it would take his mind away from Rex. "Don't you want to go?"

"Oh, sure," he answered quietly, hesitantly, more to please her, she thought after, than for his own sake. Aloisia helped Frankie into his bathing suit and then continued working at the sewing machine, thinking about how she would have to tell Louise about Rex when she came home. Fortunately, just the other day, she had taken a picture of Franz, the two children and Rex sitting on the milk stand.

Aloisia was still sitting at her sewing machine some time later when her thoughts were suddenly interrupted by the sound of running footsteps on the porch. The hired man, out of breath and looking from side to side, was at the door.

"Frankie?" His eyes quickly surveyed the room. "Frankie?" He called again. "Isn't he here?" He turned and looked out the open door again.

"Frankie is with you!"

"I don't see him. I don't see Frankie anywhere. I thought maybe he came home...?"

Aloisia bumped her chair aside and flew out the door. The two ran out past the beehives and grass lined pools, through the backfield that edged the flood-swollen slough. Tall grasses from the adjoining fields camouflaged the edges. He pointed to where Frankie had been told to wait after their dip together. He had just gone for a few minutes to visit the neighbour's wife who was sunbathing across the slough. She had waved to him. He told Frankie to wait. He would be back in a few minutes....

They kept looking around and calling, hoping to see Frankie running towards them from somewhere. They keep peering into the murky water and finally spotted a white shape as the water cleared. Joe plunged into the water and pulled up

Frankie in his arms. He looked alive but his body was motionless. The neighbour's wife, seeing that something was wrong, came running and applied artificial respiration—in vain. She ran home to telephone the doctor. Franz, seeing the commotion from the field where he was working, came too. Aloisia pleaded with Frankie to answer. Franz prayed, "I believe in God, the Father Almighty, the Creator of heaven and earth...."

Louise came home from school. Summer holidays! Frankie was waiting! She ran along Lickman Road, up their lane, across the little porch and through the open door. Everything was quiet. There was no smell of cooking. Had her mother and Frankie gone to a neighbour's farm? But they were always at home! Even Rex did not answer her call. Louise looked outside and noticed people in their backfield and a shiny black car. They had visitors! What a rare occasion! Maybe there was a party going on! She ran back inside and quickly changed into her best dress. As she ran out of the house again a police car drove into their yard. The policeman gave her a ride. What excitement! When the car stopped she jumped out. People were bending over her brother. Her parents looked up at her with bewildered eyes. Frank's body was now as cold as the snow still resting on the surrounding mountains. Aloisia wrapped her son in a large grey blanket and cradled him in her work worn arms.

The police car slowly drove back up the lane to Lickman Road and turned towards Chilliwack and the funeral home. Little Louise was thrilled that she was allowed to sit in the front seat, hardly realizing that her brother was dead, or what that meant. In the back seat, across her parents' laps, lay Frankie.

Funeral arrangements were made. A small coffin was purchased. Frankie was dressed in his new sailor's suit he was going to wear to the strawberry tea. Just that spring Franz had been very proud of how Aloisia had pieced the sailor's outfit together for both Louise and Frankie from one of his old German navy uniforms.

Word of the tragedy had spread by word of mouth at the strawberry tea. Neighbours and people Franz and Aloisia didn't even know attended the funeral. There were more than fifty bouquets of flowers. At the church Louise became the centre of attention, the centre of attention such as she had never experienced before. She smiled and giggled, not realizing that her brother was gone forever, that she would never hear herself called Idy again.

Then Louise watched in dismay as their few toys were placed into the coffin, even the red ladybug that hopped when wound up with a key. It was the last toy with which Frankie had played. The funeral cortege moved slowly east and then up the gravel road to the Little Mountain Cemetery overlooking the Fraser Valley and the snow capped mountains beyond.

Louise, who had always wanted her own bed, now slept alone under the quilt stitched together out of red and white squares and triangles, the quilt she and her brother once shared.

Only after the funeral was it realized that Frankie's drowning had been foreshadowed. Aloisia had had a dream. In it she lost one of her teeth. Its vividness was so troubling that it prompted her to describe it to a neighbour. Was there any significance to such a dream? Yes, the neighbour answered, it meant that someone was going to die. Someone she knew. Did the tooth bleed when it came out? Yes? Oh dear, then it will be someone very close to you. Aloisia thought of several relatives in Germany who had been sick for some time. Which one could it be?

Louise also had a dream that Frankie drowned in a nearby slough. A few days later, when they were riding the horse and buggy into Chilliwack, Louise pointed to the place she recognized from her dream. Everyone laughed except Frankie. He stood up and looked solemnly towards where Louise pointed.

Next day Frankie came to his mother's side as she sat at her sewing machine and said, "Mommy, do I have to die?"

"What an idea!" Aloisia looked at him in amazement. "We need good looking boys like you!" She hugged him and changed the subject.

After Frank's death Aloisia had little appetite for food. Neighbours said the hired man should be sued for negligence. He had, however, been a friend for so long. And anyway, what was the use? They couldn't get their son back.

Aloisia had difficulty sleeping. If only she had paid more attention to Frankie's reluctance, his apparent premonition. But he always liked going for a swim. Aloisia cried in anguish, "If someone would say that I could get my son back I would crawl on my hands and knees up to the cemetery." She kept imagining

Frankie walking towards her with the sack of rolled oats, asking for milk and sugar so he could have a snack.

Franz built a wooden marker and carved a cross to mount on top. Aloisia painted it white and Franz printed Frankie's name and the appropriate dates in black Gothic letters. Every Sunday, after attending Mass, they drove east to Little Mountain Cemetery to bring flowers to Frank's grave.

Aloisia miscarried. She lost the child that was going to make them a family of five before Frankie drowned.

Although Aloisia was now forty years old, she was determined to have another child. Her doctor was shocked. Look at your legs! How long is it since you tore your ligaments? And your hands are all swollen. You're too worn out. You'll just miscarry again.

It was a cold December day, December 20, 1936 to be exact. School was finished for the Christmas holidays. Louise, now nine years old, was in the kitchen. Even though it was the middle of the day, her mother had gone to bed; she was not feeling well. That was most unusual and Louise was worried. Then Franz said he had to go and get someone. Louise must go with him. He hitched up the democrat and drove up Lickman Road. He turned into a front yard, jumped out, ran to the door and knocked. A lady answered, disappeared, and immediately reappeared wearing her winter coat and carrying a large bedpan. Louise became even more worried. Why would her mother need this? When they got home again she was not allowed to go into the house; her father ordered her into the barn. "Stay there until you're called," he said firmly.

Louise was frightened. Was her mother dying? Even though she huddled in a manger and pulled hay over herself, she was cold. But her father's instructions were stern and clear. Stay in the barn until I come for you, he had said. Finally, she heard the barn door open. Her father called her name. She should come. When Louise ran into the house, the lady they had picked up was boiling something on the stove. Her father led Louise to the kitchen sofa. There was white bundle propped up on a pillow. It was a baby wrapped up in a blanket.

"This is your baby sister," he said.

"My baby sister?" Louise looked at the perfectly

formed baby.

"Yes, she's your new sister."

Soon smiling neighbours came knocking at their door. On tiptoes, Louise proudly showed off the best Christmas present that she had ever had—a living doll. Nellie Kickbush brought one of her Christmas fruitcakes as a gift. On top was a silver bell decorated with holly. Louise got a lot of attention and presents too: a bright red purse, scarf and gloves. It was wonderful to see happiness and hear laughter in a home that had experienced such a tragic loss.

"We have a new baby, we have a new baby," Louise repeated to all who were near or passed by as she walked on her tiptoes along the Chilliwack sidewalks. "Her name is Ella."

Years later (actually decades later, when it was not considered off limits to talk about pregnancy and childbirth), Aloisia explained that she had to stay at home for this birth because there was some type of women's sickness going around in the Chilliwack Hospital. The doctor said a midwife would be better for this delivery. Another detail that came out was that when Franz arrived back home with the midwife, Aloisia had already given birth—alone. When she heard the breathing and crying of her new baby she lifted the cover with her leg to be sure the baby would not suffocate, but not so much that the baby would get cold.

When Ella was a year old and Louise ten, the family drove into town for a family portrait. Franz wore the fine suit sent by Maria Kraus. Louise wore a navy blouse her mother had made and a big white bow in her hair. The family portrait turned out very well; the baby in Aloisia's arms was holding up her right hand, her fingers in the sign of peace. Franz said he had seen a painting called "The Infant Jesus of Prague" in which the Christ Child held his fingers in exactly the same manner. He said it was a good omen.

By the following year, the frugality of the Baumgartner family allowed them to save enough money to buy a fifty-five acre farm on 550 Prairie Central Road in East Chilliwack. It would be a new beginning. The farm, built by Chilliwack pioneer, Jacob Zink, had been rented for several years but now was for sale. The land was flat. The soil was neither full of stones as in Broadwater nor was it clay as in Achlitz. It was peat and easy to till. The barn was massive with two rows of milking stations for twenty-four cows. There was space at the end of one row to tether a bull, separate pens for calves, three stalls for horses and an area for mixing the fodder. Nobody had to pump water anymore. It was piped right to the mangers! All the barn needed was a good cleaning, sweeping out the cobwebs and whitewashing. The huge silo? Well, Franz didn't have much use for silage; he believed it wasn't needed to produce milk both high in quality and quantity. He had already proven that in Achlitz. Some day he would dismantle it, using the lumber to build an implement shed for their plough, harrow, seeder, hay wagon and all the other equipment essential for running a farm.

The house, though very small, had running water too. In fact, they could see Elk Creek Falls, the source of the water supply, right from the window above the kitchen sink.

Franz and Aloisia made plans to enlarge the small house. Of course it would be wood frame— that was how good farmhouses were built in the Fraser Valley—with a covered veranda across the front. Franz and Aloisia were not actually planning to sit on the veranda; there was too much work to do. The veranda would look good though. And it was the style. Between it and the road would be her flower garden: gladiolas, red roses, a yellow climber, a purple clematis (Aloisia would dig them up from the old place in Achlitz—nobody would miss them).

Off the kitchen would be a separate living room. And that is where Aloisia would find a special place for the family picture that had turned out so well. They would wallpaper above the wainscoting. The paint would be enamel. No more calcimine.

A short hallway from the kitchen would lead past a bathroom that had a toilet and a bathtub and a sink—yes, all three! Near the end of the hall on the right hand side were two bedrooms. One had to go through the smaller one to get to the parent's bedroom.

At the very end of the hall a door would lead to the storage part of the house: a storage cellar (no more root house like in Broadwater with bears sniffing around) with sturdy shelves laden with jars of purple, gold and red fruit; crocks of sauerkraut and dill pickles and bins for potatoes and Russet apples and an area where Franz could store his barrels of homemade apple cider.

There was also a room to store various beekeeping paraphernalia and separate honey from the wax

(Aloisia would bring her bees, of course).

The area to the right would all be left wide open for the storage of wood (mostly birch and alder) cut from the small forest left at the back of the farm. The cascara trees that they noticed when they inspected the property would be the source of extra income; the bark could be peeled and sold to Buckerfields for medicinal purposes.

There would also be a second floor with two dormers to let in both the morning and afternoon sun. When all was complete, Aloisia would gently wash and starch her old white lace curtains and unpack the ones from the Old Country that she had never had a chance to use.

At the back of the house a sliding door would open to the farmyard with its path past the chicken house to the barn (the outhouse was still there and handy when working outside).

They would plant a larger orchard: Gravenstein Apples, Italian Prunes, Bartlett Pears and Bing Cherries—all their favorites—and a row of grapes along one side screening the row of beehives.

Louise, now eleven years old, could walk to the East Chilliwack Elementary School; it was only two miles along a gravel road well maintained with a grader.

Little Ella would walk the same route in a few years.

The mailbox was on the road right in front of their house. One of the first things Franz did when they moved was to paint the address and the family name in handsome black, Gothic letters. *BAUMGARTNER*. It was 1938. Not bad progress considering they had arrived in Canada only eleven years before with no money. They had survived. Neighbours were amazed as the Fraser Valley Milk Producer's truck picked up more cans of milk. The humble farmhouse had been transformed into a beautiful country home with wooden siding painted white. There was an orchard on one side; a well kept vegetable garden on the other and flowers reaching from the front verandah right to the road. Aloisia and Franz took pictures with their box camera and mailed them to family back home.

The economy was doing well in Germany too. People from all over the world were investing there. They said Hitler really knew how to make a country hum. Aloisia often felt she should have stayed in the Old Country with her family, but now her son's grave was here.

Franz didn't trust Hitler and knew that as long

as he was in power, Germany was not a safe country for him. He wouldn't go back, even if he had the money to spare.

When the Second World War broke out German immigrants were subject to ridicule. One day the local co-op didn't pick up their flats of raspberries; somebody had sprinkled lime on them. They had to go into the Chilliwack police station regularly to report that they were still in the area. Rumours circulated that Franz was communicating directly with Hitler using radio equipment secretly installed in his silo. Franz tore the silo down. It was never used anyway and he had always meant to use the lumber for building an implement shed.

But the psychological stresses from war were not as simple to overcome as the physical act of tearing down a silo. The fact that his fatherland was once again plunged into war deeply disturbed Franz. He was troubled by international politics and obsessed by news on the radio. He became increasingly restless. He started studying his Esperanto notes again—the ones he had made in his youth. He talked of egalitarianism, dreamed of being free, of travelling back to Argentina where he had lived as a young man. He didn't need a wife. Being a husband, a father, even a farmer, meant less and less to him. That was really made clear when a cattle truck came to load up his dairy cows for the Chilliwack auction.

By the time the Second World War was over, so was their marriage.

In later years, Aloisia said that if the war had not come along they could have made it. Yes, war can destroy so much.

The Swing

A dairy farm in East Chilliwack was the location of my first childhood memories. Beside our house was an orchard where robins built nests in cherry, apple, plum and pear trees. When the eggs hatched the adults fed their young with grubs and earthworms scratched from the nearby raspberry patch.

Just next to this scene was my secret world under a huge weeping willow tree. Rays of sunshine played tag with minnows, water spiders and tadpoles in the adjacent small ditch. On the other side there was a gravel road. Sometimes the crescendo of an automobile or tractor would approach. After passing, the sweet smell of dust floated through my curtain shadow of willow leaves. The driver didn't even realize that I was watching.

What made this secret world so special was the swing my father had built for me. If I pumped hard I could reach high among the willow branches. If I jerked the ropes I was on a boat on rough seas. Twisting the ropes made me dizzy as they unwound. But these were things any ordinary swing could do.

However, this was no ordinary swing with two ropes attached to one board. My father had nailed four boards together making a sturdy wooden rectangle that had to be suspended with four ropes. Because of the unique design of this swing I could walk around the edges as if I were on a trapeze platform or a flying carpet. I made golden chains of dandelions to enhance the performance. My cat, Jingi, was usually watching as she lay in the tall grasses near by.

Sometimes this swing was an escape from the tension in my parents' marriage. An example was the aftermath of when my mother tried to get her driver's license. She was in the driver's seat of our Model T Ford; my father was beside her and my sister, Louise, and I were in the back seat. As my mother drove, the tires touched the loose gravel on the shoulder and my father got upset, accusing her of counting the cows in the neighbour's field and not paying attention to the road. He grabbed the steering wheel but jerked it too much to the left and the car swerved across the road and slid down into the adjacent slough. We all crawled out the side windows not yet submerged in water and scrambled up the embankment. Thank goodness, no one was hurt.

A tow truck was called and pulled the car up the bank. Our sturdy Model T had suffered no real exterior damage. However from that time on a mouldy smell emanated from the velour upholstery—those areas that had been soaked in the muddy water. My mother was hoping that now my dad would buy a new car. He had the money, she said. But he said no. And that was the end of mother's driving lessons.

In the meantime, Louise had moved into New Westminster for nurse's training. She became aware of a better life and told mother that nobody should put up with so much work—work that wasn't even appreciated while my father often drove into Chilliwack to talk with the locals about the world situation, etc.

A sympathetic neighbour told my sister she had a brother who had bought a house in Burnaby. He was a bachelor and could spare a room—and some storage space. Mother and I could move into his house until she bought her own place. While my parent's separation agreement was worked out, swinging under the willow tree made me feel safe and sheltered me from the details of an unknown future.

The Swing

When I opened our back door after the two mile walk home from East Chilliwack Elementary School, my Mother was seldom in the house. I would make myself some junket, adding plenty of sugar, before going outside to look for her. She might be feeding the pigs, or in the chicken house, or in the barn caring for a newborn calf, or checking the beehives. She might be helping my father clear trees and brush in the small forest out back beyond the fields.

My father would haul the stumps together into huge piles using a horse and tackle. It was my mother's job to find dry materials to start the fire. Then, poking and pushing the burning stumps with a long sturdy stick, or crowbar if necessary, she worked around the pile until all that was left were ashes and a few smoldering embers. She would come home with singed eyebrows but never complained as it was one of her most enjoyable chores. Even years later she insisted that burning stump piles was her favourite occupation, even restful, she would say.

That's where Mom was, at the stump fires, when the report of the war's end came over the kitchen radio. Victory at last!

My sister wrote the news on a slip of paper and folded it into my hand. "Never forget this day," she said, holding up her finger for emphasis. "Give this to Mom and Dad. It's very important. Run!" Happy to be entrusted with such an important errand, I ran out the back door and along the cow paths where the soft summer dust caressed my feet until I reached the bush which my parents were clearing.

"So that is why the neighbour has been hammering on the ploughshare for the last half hour," they said, looking at each other. Usually that gong was only used to announce lunch or dinner.

My mother was always working, though perhaps I shouldn't say 'always' as once I found her sitting in the kitchen doing some darning. I remember it so well because it was a shock to see her sitting quietly and resting. With a slightly embarrassed look on her sun-freckled face, and wearing a clean cotton print dress that looked like a Jack and Jill illustration, she explained that she had torn the ligaments in her legs. She had slipped off the ladder on the hay wagon, and Dad had to drive her the five and a half miles into Chilliwack to see the doctor. No bones were broken, but for the first time that I can remember, my mother would have to rest.

One day a long cattle truck drove into our yard. The barn swallows watched while apprehensive black and white Holsteins were herded up the ramps to be transported for auction. Only one cow called Gelbe, was kept. The horses stayed too.

Inside the house there was the scraping sound of empty and full cardboard boxes being pushed across linoleum floors. Mother carefully wrapped objects which she had brought to this country as a bride.

That Friday my sister came from the city to help. The next morning a moving truck slowly turned off the road, crossed our log bridge and drove down our driveway. Exhaust fumes sputtered out as it carefully maneuvered around the barnyard and slowly backed up through a part of the fence that was seldom opened, stopping at the back door of our farmhouse.

My mother, sister and the driver quickly loaded chests, drawers and dismantled beds onto the truck. Rosie, my old doll was tucked safely under my arm. Strong ropes were tied across the back of the truck. We were ready to leave. My mother sat next to the driver. I sat next to the door that was still open.

My father walked towards us. He must have been watching. Did he want to say something to me?

"Don't pay any attention to him. Pull the door shut," my mother said sternly as the driver turned on the ignition. My father put his hand on the door frame so I could not close the door.

"Pull the door shut," my mother said again, determined and cold.

After a moment, my dad dropped his hand and the door closed easily. I looked away, never knowing what he was going to say.

The truck drove through the gate, across the bridge and along the gravel road passing my favourite swing under the weeping willow tree. I didn't realize at the time that this was the end of my childhood and I would never see the farm again.

The Swing

The truck stopped just up the road, dropping me off at my best friend, Gail's, home where my mother had made arrangements for me to stay until I completed my grade seven in Chilliwack Junior High School. During all that time, whenever I walked past our farm to take the bus to school my father never came out to say hello. It would be another fifteen years before I would have any meaningful contact with my father.

When I finally joined my mother in Burnaby, I attended the New Westminster Junior High School, the largest high school in Canada at the time (I still have bad dreams about wandering down endless hallways). I changed from a thin, anemic child to a healthy, if slightly overweight young teen. I reported to my shocked mother that a classmate had told me I looked pregnant. Looking at myself in my mother's dresser mirror, I realized she was right. I tried pulling in my stomach, but in the end my puppy fat soon disappeared.

My teacher, trying to help me overcome my shyness, gave me a comedy role in a school play. I received an award as the student who had made the most improvement in one year. My mother arranged to take me out of school a little early so we could visit her relatives in Germany whom she had not seen for twenty years. My teacher gave me a delicate, round, rose-covered handkerchief as a going away gift.

When we returned from our trip, my mother bought a craftsman style house in New Westminster. It was close to the bus service which was important because my mother never did learn how to drive.

Upstairs there was a little suite with a small kitchen built into the dormer overlooking the back yard which she rented out. On the main floor the dining room and sun porch became our bedrooms. Her sewing machine hid behind the kitchen door. The living room remained a living room, but the two bedrooms were rented out.

My mother asked me to print 'Room and Board' on a piece of cardboard which she placed in a front window. At first, the words seemed strange, but I soon understood their meaning. There never was a vacancy for any length of time; the aroma of bay leaves, nutmeg and cinnamon advertised her good cooking. The rooms and linens were always fresh and clean. Word of mouth kept the rooms occupied, so she eventually took the sign down.

Gradually she built three additional bedrooms in the basement with a sink and toilet built in a corner and installed hotplates so renters could do their own cooking. The remaining area was for a washing machine and tubs. When it rained this part of the basement was filled with bedding and laundry hanging from lines.

My mother was always friendly. Nobody could be in her kitchen for more than a few minutes without being offered coffee and homemade cookies or cake. The conversation around our kitchen table was always interesting as tenants related stories about their lives.

My mother shared her past experiences too, especially those concerning my father and Broadwater, the place where she spent her first two years of marriage. She often recounted the story of disembarking the train in Nelson and getting married the next morning. She would share how difficult life had been when she came from the Old Country as nothing in Franz' letters had ever indicated that she would be living in an isolated hunter's shack that wouldn't 'even be used for pigs' in her village back in Germany, a shack that was 'hanging on the side of a mountain' as she used to say. She had been stunned to see that a rolled up piece of corrugated sheet metal served as the chimney for a miniature cast iron stove. There was no place to store her linens or the other household supplies she had so carefully packed when leaving her home in Bavaria. Water had to be carried in pails along a mountain path from a spring. Bears, wolves and cougars were her neighbours, not people. She felt she had been tricked.

In those days it wasn't enough to say you were separated because you didn't get along with each other, or that he had some shortcomings. The general consensus was that if a man strayed or was difficult in any way it was really the wife's fault. Unless, of course, he were dead. And for the first few months in New Westminster she had told everyone she was a widow. I was glad when my father started to make the occasional visit because I didn't like the lie.

Mother would confide with each new tenant how hard life had been on the farm, explaining how they logged to make telephone poles even though she was already pregnant.

More and more, the mundane every day farm chores had been left to my mother. She said that after they moved to the Fraser Valley my father liked to go around selling the honey from her bees as this gave him a chance to discuss politics. He spoke English well, often using words such as 'egalitarianism' and 'hypocrisy'.

My dad liked going to auctions. Sometimes he bought a horse for just a few dollars, a horse that nobody else wanted. He came home very pleased with himself, while mom had done all the milking alone...again. When the truck arrived in the yard and the poor beast was encouraged down the ramp to our barnyard, its dazed look matched that of my mother's as she shook her head in dismay. But my father would inevitably nurse the animal back to health until it became a good workhorse, hardly recognizable from when it had first arrived.

One of the biggest embarrassments for my mother occurred in the Chilliwack churchyard one Sunday when the Roman Catholic archbishop was visiting St. Mary's Church. My father had gone to him for confession and told him that he had practiced his conjugal rights without intending to have children. The archbishop had admonished my father. When mass was over my father cornered the archbishop in the churchyard and in a voice loud enough for all parishioners around to hear, he said that if having children was so important the archbishop should have some himself.

My father said he wanted his freedom. Maybe he would even travel back to Argentina where he had pioneered before coming to Canada and marrying my mother. He worked hard enough building up their dairy farm but there was never an end—there was always more to do. The farm was all paid for; there were no debts and, thanks to the hard work of both my mother and my sister, he rarely needed a hired man. My mother said he had enough money to buy property in town as an investment. Instead, he now spent more and more time standing in the little bit of wilderness still left at the back of the farm with pencil and note pad in hand writing poetry.

In private, he would sometimes call the British, 'the Brutish' for what had done in Argentina before he immigrated to Canada. They offered bounties for the scalps of natives; double if the hunters shot a pregnant woman. WWII was raging while we were on the farm and as German immigrants my parents had to report weekly to the RCMP in town so that the government always knew where we were.

I listened with love and patience as my mother complained endlessly about my father to her tenants, but I got more and more uncomfortable with this topic. I protested. I hated hearing bad things about my father. However, she insisted, "Did your father ever do anything for you? Did he send you anything for your graduation? No! I put your graduation picture in the Chilliwack newspaper. He must have seen it as he's always writing articles and letters to the editor."

After I got married, my husband and I bought a house in the Queens Park area of New Westminster. Her rebukes continued on the telephone.

"Mom, please stop it! I can't take it anymore. I know it was terrible. We all know how much you suffered and we're sorry."

"You're just too sensitive," was her habitual reply.

Finally, I threatened to hang up if she continued. She continued.

I put the receiver down. I felt as though a rat was eating a piece of my soul. But after that our conversations were usually about other topics.

Once our two children began going to school, I befriended some of the elderly people in the rooming houses on Townsend Place bringing them flowers from our garden. Where were their relatives? Why were they alone?

Then memories of my father started to surface. I recalled the time my girlfriend and I crouched on the back roof and sprinkled leaves on his head as he stepped out the door. He just looked up smiling and continued walking. He didn't even get mad. I remembered that he built me a four-sided swing and once he made me a pair of stilts that he painted a bright red. He helped me write a book report on the children's story, Pit Pony. And he showed me how to select carrots for a vegetable competition, "Don't pick the best, pick the most uniform." He also explained the meaning behind many expressions such as, *'a stitch in time saves nine'*.

My father had been a signaler in the German

Navy during World War One and taught me the first few letters of the alphabet. I memorized up to the letter "G" before my interest waned. He also told me the secret of his excellent cider was to select only the best apples and wash them first before putting them through the press, saying, "Some people don't even start out properly."

I remembered the time he told me to do something although my mother had just an hour earlier given me a different order. (In retrospect, I think I was daring to play one parent against the other.) "Who should I obey?" I asked him in confusion. "Always the last order," he answered quietly, "The situation might have changed."

I decided to contact my father but I didn't tell my mother as she would have been hurt. One day, I built up the courage to call the operator in Chilliwack and get his phone number. With a name like Baumgartner—the only one in the area—the number was quickly found.

"Hello Dad? This is Ella."

"Who?"

"Ella, your daughter."

Silence. I almost thought we were disconnected. "And what do you want after all these years?"

"I just wanted to know how you were, Dad. I thought you might like to meet your grandchildren."

Silence. "Well, I'll have to think about it. You can't just jump into my life and expect me to be thrilled after all these years."

"Yes," I answered softly, "I know. I understand."

Not long after a letter arrived from him, full of bitterness. He had strong reservations about resuming contact...at this time. My reply included some photographs of his grandchildren and invited him for a visit. Finally, he replied that yes, he would take the bus to the New Westminster station close to our home.

As the date approached, I carefully cleaned the house. The hands of the clock ticked the time down to the moment when I would see my father again. Screened by the living room curtains, I watched for him. Then suddenly I saw him walking up the shaded sidewalk wearing a gray fedora and carrying an old leather bag, his erect bearing and gait the same as I remembered from years ago.

I welcomed him at the door.

My father looked at me rather gravely and shaking my hand said, "Hello Ella." He was carefully shaven and impeccably dressed even though I knew he bought all his clothes from thrift stores. Both my parents had always done this.

He interacted pleasantly with my husband. Reaching into his pocket, he pulled out a small black coin purse, snapped it open and gave a few pennies to each of the children.

Then he lifted the leather bag he had been carrying onto the kitchen table and took out a package wrapped in newspaper. Could it be something for me? I could not remember ever receiving a gift from him before. Out of the wrappings emerged an old brown bean crock the shape and colour of a huge chestnut. I cradled it in my hands and felt its smooth chubby handle. The lid's edge was a little chipped. Who knows in which second hand store he found it or to whom the crock once belonged? It didn't matter. I was used to such things. In fact, I had learned to treasure objects that were old or damaged. It was mine now, so fat and round and heavy, a gift from my father.

But I didn't bake beans. That wasn't a favorite recipe in our family. When he left I put it on display on a shelf in the kitchen, out of the way.

One afternoon I discovered a recipe for red cabbage in a French cookbook, Choux Rouges a la Flamande. It required Russet apples. And we had a Russet tree right in our backyard, leaning towards an equally weathered pear tree planted in pioneer times. It was late autumn and the Russets had had the sweetening touch of the first frost. Wind, rain and woodpeckers had knocked many to the ground.

The children and I dressed warmly and went outside. Long shadows from old fruit trees, the children's swing and neighbouring houses mingled with our shadows and laughter. The loden green Russets were scattered here and there among the damp pungent leaves. We put them in a basket with rope handles and carried them up the stairs into the kitchen.

I lifted the crock down from the shelf . It was what the recipe called for, an earthenware crock It was heavy and I realized for the first time what a weight it must have been for my father to carry it all the way up the hill from the bus stop on that first visit.

I washed it and carefully dried it. Using my hand I generously covered the inside with fresh butter. The red cabbage was shredded and put in along with brown sugar, salt, pepper, nutmeg and cider vinegar. I gently placed the lid on the filled crock and placed it into the oven, on low heat.

After about an hour peeled and quartered Russets were added. Soon they were tender. A stir and little more salt and pepper and it was done. The delicious aroma of cooked red cabbage filled the kitchen. Our whole family enjoyed it.

As a child, I rarely received gifts and certainly never anything brand new from a department store, wrapped with ribbons and a fancy tag. Used flour sacks became undershirts. The clothes that my mother couldn't cut down from other clothes all came from thrift stores like the Salvation Army. Heaven knows where she got the dark blue flannel to make my bloomers, a constant embarrassment when I had to use the common outhouse behind the school. The jumper that appears in one of my school photos was khaki-coloured, probably Army surplus material. My mother embroidered two large yellow daisies on each of the front straps trying to hide the seams necessitated by the shortage of material but the straps still looked pieced together.

One Christmas, I remember getting a doll that I had been looking for since the previous summer. It was in a doll bed that my mother had hammered together from some scrap wood and varnished herself. She had sewn some linen for it too. What could I say? She was trying so hard to save money. As usual, there was no gift from my father.

Once when I was playing in the crawl space under the front porch of our farmhouse where mother kept her beanpoles, I found a long piece of wood that looked like a rifle with a knothole serving as the trigger. I was very excited—a free gun! Not that I had ever really wanted a gun of any kind. I showed it to my parents who were not impressed as their families had both suffered from war and strongly felt that guns—even toy guns—should not be encouraged. Canada was in middle of WWII (another war to end all wars?) and so my wooden rifle disappeared very quickly.

On later visits my father showed my children how to eat with a knife and fork. Another time he stood on one leg and then, giving strange bird-like chirps, danced a little jig. He said that even old people should have fun and pretend to be children sometimes. As an example, he put the hand of one arm under his other armpit and then pumped his arm up and down to make a loud squeaky noise.

After that first visit my father visited quite regularly and he always had some gift. Once it was a small piece of porcelain, a boy and girl not over two inches high, in the softest hues of pink and gold. They were cuddled together, fast asleep. Whatever they had been leaning on was missing. On the back, my father had carefully written with indelible pencil:

This is a part of another part.
To know what it was, you must be smart.

When I noticed that the words were fading, I carefully traced over what he had written so many years before.

Once an old Chinese ceramic vase emerged from a spare sweater he had brought in case the weather got cooler. He carefully placed it on our kitchen counter. It was almost a foot high. Though I had never studied Oriental art, I appreciated the beautiful colours! Powder blue, magenta, forest green and cinnamon figures on horseback seemed to be playing some kind of game on an ivory background. There was a little piece broken from the lip but I eventually filled it with putty and stained it with dark brown shoe polish. You can hardly even see where there was once a missing piece.

On another visit he reached into the pocket of his large winter coat and pulled out a shaving mug. It was cream coloured and age had given it a crackle effect. In shades of moss green were glazed miniature lattices, roses and the following words:

CRÈME de SAVON
pour la barbe.
ROGER & GALLET
Paris, France

It rests on my bathroom counter next to an antique vase of the same colours and an oval, ivory hand mirror which I had picked up at a garage sale for one dollar. I was told that the mirror was once part of a trousseau brought from Scotland before the turn of the nineteenth century. The three together make a lovely arrangement.

My father also gave me a little two inch high grey enamel cup with a thin black rim that he had carried with him while living in the jungles of Argentina. He had used it to drink from the crystal clear streams there, the best water he had ever tasted. It was while he was pioneering in Argentina that he had received a letter from his father wrote asking him to return home and help out on the family farm. He packed his belongings and sailed home thinking he would be able to use the knowledge he had gained at agricultural college, but once he got home his father insisted on doing everything the old fashioned way. When my father wanted to get his suit cleaned or complained about the outhouse being full of cobwebs, his father exploded in anger, "Who do you think you are with all your fancy ideas?"

My mother, who at that time had been corresponding with my father for almost a decade, was hoping the situation would be resolved. She had visited the family farm once and admitted that what Franz had written to her was true. The farm was not well run. She imagined herself married and helping Franz bring the family farm into shape, but my father felt that it would be fruitless and signed away his rights of primogenitor to his younger brother.

In any case, my father was opposed to the National Socialist Party ideas and had to flee Germany when he shouted, "You're not democratic!" during one of Hitler's speeches in Munich. Escaping over the border to Switzerland, he carried cheese produced in an alpine hut down to the valley below and brought bread and sausages back up to the workers above.

He returned to his village of Eggersham in Germany just long enough to gather his belongings with the intention of sailing back to South America where he had come to know and respect the indigenous people. However, an acquaintance gave him new and promising information about Canada being a better destination. So, my father decided to emigrate there. He hoped that my mother would come with him, but her family vehemently opposed the idea of her giving up what she had for a very uncertain future. And who did he think he was anyway, expecting her to leave her well-established life for a man who was not even from her area but from the other side of Bavaria? Saddened, but determined to leave Germany, he emigrated to Canada alone. A year later despite her family's objections, Aloisia joined him in Nelson, British Columbia.

I recall my father arriving with a huge shopping bag. On top there was a piece of cardboard with his beautiful handwriting, 'German Navy Uniform

1916'. This is the only gift for which I actually took up the courage to request. I said who else would appreciate it more? And now here it was. First he took out his navy hat. It had a black band on front of which was embossed in gold serif letters, S.M.S. Friedrich der Grosse, which was the flagship of the German Navy. Two black ribbons hung from the back. There was a bundle of navy collars each properly folded and tied—except for one that was loose so it could be inspected. There was a necktie, carefully knotted and ready to be slipped on over the head. He said he had sewn it himself from his mother's black silk scarf. It was formed with a very special knot. It shouldn't be untied; I would probably never find anyone to tie it properly again. In a small wooden cigar box there were special buttons and crests that indicated he had some authority, had been a signaler, had promised nine years of service.

On subsequent visits we labeled everything carefully so I wouldn't forget. At a later date he gave a brass seal with the initials FB that he used for closing envelopes with wax. He also gave me the small brass compass he used in the navy.

And he told me stories about his experiences

at sea. Once, he said, the men were having a party. Women were on board and there was a lot of drinking. Most people have no morals, he said. He kept to himself as he wasn't one of them.

Once when he was on lookout he saw in the distance the telltale ripple of a torpedo coming right at his ship. His eyesight was so good that even with the naked eye he could often see better than most people with binoculars. He set off the alarm. His ship was able to turn just in time for the white streak of the torpedo to pass them by.

"Yes, I saved a thousand lives that day," he said. I thought the large number was really impossible. Was he exaggerating? But later research confirmed that figure. As a reward he could attend a university in Munich. Further research also confirmed something else he told me: some of the sailors used roller skates to get around on that huge ship.

He had a reputation for having a loud voice. Without any apparent effort he could open his mouth and shout as loud as though using a megaphone. Fellow seamen called him Tarzan.

On one visit Dad told us that BC Hydro had contacted him as they were consolidating land along the Columbia River that would be affected by a new dam. They offered him more than he could ever have imagined for his isolated Broadwater homestead. I felt a lump forming in my throat as I had always imagined my parents' thirty-three acre site as a future place for family holidays. I told him what I was thinking. He didn't say anything, just frowned a little and closed his eyes the way he did sometimes when mulling over something in his mind.

Shortly afterwards, he mailed me a copy of a letter he had sent to Hydro. It stated that I should have the first right to repurchase the thirty-three acres at Broadwater after the flooding was complete.

As things turned out, despite my many efforts to reclaim my parent's old homestead, the property was turned into a provincial park. Probably the best thing in the end.

My father passed away after one of the many visits he made. Every time I used the old crock he had given me, I thought of him. And it's still just like new. Or more exactly, its just like when my Father first carefully unwrapped it from pieces of newspaper, smiled, and handed it to me over thirty years ago.

The Old Navy Uniform

On one of Dad's visits to New Westminster I showed him a photograph of him wearing a navy uniform. I had found it in an old album of my mother's.

"Yes, that was me," he said matter-of-factly. "I was the signaler on the flag ship of the German Navy."

It seemed unreal that my father who loved trees and meadows so much had to live separate from these things. But it was true. How he got conscripted or why he chose this career rather than some other aspect of serving his country, I didn't think of asking at the time. And he didn't tell me. Or if I did, I have forgotten. Anyway it's hard to remember things you don't understand and my knowledge or, for that matter, my interest in the circumstances surrounding the outbreak of WWI was virtually non-existent at the time.

I do remember hearing that after the war when he got back home he liked to wander under the trees and across the fields to the despair of some of the other family members who felt he should only work, eat, and sleep. It was probably a relief for him to look up at trees with leaves rather than masts where ropes and metal took the place of branches and foliage.

Once he showed me some of the alphabet he learned as a signaler. He used pieces of a flour sack that mom bleached on the grass behind our house until they were almost white. I say almost because some colors didn't bleach out despite repeated spraying with the water hose and exposure to weeks of sunshine. These she used for making undershirts, pillowcases and dish towels. Anyway it was two pieces of white cloth attached to a couple of sticks that he used to demonstrate the signaler's alphabet behind our house. "This is the letter A and this is B...." he continued through the alphabet. Finally he flashed out some words and sentences.

I had visions of using this sign language with my friend Gail who lived just down the road. We could carry out secret conversations. I only learned A to G, however. Then I guess it all became too complicated. Memorizing was not my forte and Dad didn't push the matter. In retrospect, I realize he must have been a top student at the naval academy to be selected for the flagship of the German navy, and be given the training and the responsibility of being a signaler.

"Is it true," I asked, "That you saved the men on your ship by spotting a torpedo? I think I remember mom mentioned that once."

"Yes, that's true. All the men were having a party and doing a lot of drinking. There were even women on board. Most people have no morals, you know. But I wasn't one of them. I kept to myself. I was on lookout. Everyone was half drunk from the partying. Anyway, I was the only one that saw the ripple of a torpedo coming right at the ship. I had such good eyes I could see with the naked eye better than most men could see with binoculars. I set off the alarm and our ship turned just in time to see the white streak of the torpedo pass by."

"I guess everyone was happy with the close miss," I added hoping for more information but not knowing the right questions to ask.

"Yes, I saved over a thousand lives that day. Got a reward."

"So many sailors were on the ship?" I asked incredulously.

He nodded, but in my heart I thought the figure rather incredulous. However I learned in later years that his ship, Frederick the Great, had 41 officers and 1043 enlisted men on board. I also learned from my dad's niece that the reward was an admission to university in Munich. This is one of the locations from which he wrote my mother.

What I didn't realize, until years later, was that as a signaler he had to climb up to the crow's nest. Of course he had to be up there in all weather. Windy, freezing cold. My mother told me he almost froze to death one time. His superiors thought he was so strong that he could take anything. Years later he had trouble keeping warm and had to go to bed wearing several woolen coats. When he suffered from rheumatism he would whip his back with stinging nettles. It seemed to relieve the pain.

"I still have my old navy suit."

"Your old navy suit that you actually wore in WWI?"

"Certainly," he said.

I thought for a while. I had never asked him for anything before. He just brought things that he found attractive and thought I might appreciate such as the bean crock, the little shaving mug and the porcelain twins he had found at the Salvation Army or other thrift stores. I asked him if he would consider giving me his old navy uniform. "Who would appreciate it more?" I asked. "A stranger wouldn't even know to whom it belonged."

He closed his eyes as though he were going to sleep, but the furrows moving on his forehead indicated that he was thinking, concentrating, figuring something out. Then he opened them and said, "That might be a good idea, if you want it."

"I would love it," I said.

Some weeks latter my dad brought a very large brown shopping bag. He asked if he could put it on the dining room table. He took out a piece of cardboard on which was written in his beautiful handwriting *German Navy Uniform 1916*. Right on top was his navy hat with a black band and two long ribbons that hung from the back. He took it out and carefully turned it to expose the front on which was embossed in gold serif letters *S.M.S. Friedrich der Grosse*. He gently placed his hat on the table and spread the ribbons out to one side. Then he took out a bundle of navy collars, each properly folded and tied, except for one. It was loose so it could be inspected.

There was also a necktie carefully knotted and ready to be slipped on. My dad had sewn it himself from a black silk scarf given to him by his mother. He said it was a very special knot and shouldn't be untied because I would probably never find anyone to put it together again. So I didn't. There were special buttons and crests that showed that he had some authority, had been a signaler and had promised nine years of service.

On subsequent visits we neatly labeled everything so I wouldn't forget. And he told me some anecdotes about the ship being so big men sometimes used roller skates to get around. He said he became famous for his loud voice. Without apparent effort he could open his mouth and shout as though using a megaphone. The men called him Tarzan.

One day I asked him if he would to try on his old navy suit. It fit quite well after almost half a century. He solemnly saluted as I photographed him.

The Resting Place

L ooking for something?" The voice came from behind the trees.

Startled, we turned to see a woman walking towards us. "No, no. Just looking at the periwinkle," I said.

"On private property? Do you know you're on private property? This is our back yard."

"Your back yard? Doesn't it belong to the cemetery?" my husband asked.

"No, it's private."

"Isn't this part of Little Mountain Cemetery?" I said. "There used to be just wilderness right up the mountainside. I noticed the subdivision going up but I thought these trees were still part of the cemetery."

A chipmunk chattered, protesting our intrusion into the shadowy silence.

The woman tilted her head and squinted. "Weren't you here before? A couple of years ago? I came out but you were gone."

"Yes, that must have been us. We don't come that often. Things sure have changed. There used to be a shed there," I said, pointing to a bare patch of ground between the forest and where the gravestones started. "It was green. I think it had shovels and things for the caretakers."

"Yes, a real eyesore. People were always throwing junk behind it and did their business, if you know what I mean. We finally got the cemetery people to take it down last year."

I looked around. Still no bathroom facilities. When I was a little girl I used go behind the shed.

The woman pointed to a granite block nearby. "Is that yours?"

"Yes, my father's ashes. My mother's grave is just over there, " I said nodding towards the sunlit graveyard. "It was a long time ago."

I remembered the knock on our door late one

night. Two police officers informed me of my father's death. It was May and he probably wanted to do some gardening, they said. He was in his back yard. He was wearing gumboots. The doctor said it was instant—a heart attack. The calendar inside his door was crossed off three days before. Was it possible? His last letter had just arrived. On the envelope was a blue post office label that said 'perishable'. A pressed wisteria blossom, still fragrant, was tucked inside the letter.

A few weeks later a cardboard box, only about six inches square, arrived at the door. It was my father's ashes—all that was left of his strong body.

I placed the box high up on a shelf in our entrance hall closet. Where would be a suitable burial site? Many possibilities came to mind. Should his ashes be buried at sea? He had been a signaler on a German flagship. But he was not a seaman by choice. He preferred looking up at the branches of trees rather than the masts of his ship. I remember him joyfully showing me a huge tree near his home that both of us, stretching as much as possible, could not get our arms around. That tree was so big.

Before we had our alarm system we had a

number of break-ins. One time a burglar spotted the box and started taking it away. He dropped it on our stairway and when we got home there were my father's ashes on the floor. I mended the box and carefully placed my father's ashes back in it.

Still I couldn't think of a suitable place for them. Then my mother passed away. She was buried in the cemetery on top of the Chilliwack Little Mountain beside her son who had drowned so many years before. I decided to place my father's ashes in the forest just a few steps from her grave. He would be close to her, yet on his own or *'Free'* as he liked to say. All of the family agreed with this idea.

One sunny morning my sister and I drove to Chilliwack and up to the cemetery. Mother's grave was always easy to find; just follow the path leading to the green shed. After trimming around the headstone, we arranged baby's breath and love-in-a-mist in the container there. We had brought them from home. They were two of her favourite flowers.

Then I carried my father's ashes a few steps into the forest. We placed the box into a hole and covered it with the surrounding humus soil that had built up over the years from evergreens and birches. I planted some periwinkle plants I had brought from home.

My sister brought water from the tap at the end of the pathway. Then she looked around. "A stone of some kind would be good. Something to mark the place."

We walked to the back of the shed where there was always an assortment of boards, jars, discarded bouquets and wreaths. A granite block was jutting out from beneath some two-by-fours. We pried it out. Only one word was engraved on it in large Gothic letters: *FATHER.* My sister and I looked at each other in amazement. It was a sign of approval. We rolled it over to the periwinkle.

"Could you take it away?" the woman's voice brought me back to the present. "It's probably heavy." She looked at my husband. "But I really wish you would."

"Yes, yes," my husband said. "It is your back yard." He lifted the granite block up and placed it in the trunk of our car. We brought it home.

What should I do with it? For a while it served as a step into our ravine. I thought my father would have liked that. But when we had a slide in our back yard a few years later it clung to the edge of the forest barely avoiding rolling all the way down to the creek. Then I put it under the water tap and placed my mother's old galvanized watering can on it. There, however, it was always in the way. For some years now it holds up one end of a heavy plank bench on the shady side of our house.

I'm glad the periwinkle took root.

Too Sentimental

My father knew that I was very sentimental about Broadwater. One day, he wrote me this poem:

Two soldiers travelled all alone
After the bloody war was done,
Defeated, home to far off kins,
On foot, that was their only means.

It was old Joe and his pal George
Crossing a water-filled steep gorge.
When Joe said to his younger friend:
"You know what I have in mind?

The mighty plank on which we walked
Above the rushing cataract

*Would be a lovely souvenir.
I plan to move it and stay here."*

*Smart George got home, caressed the bride.
Joe pulled the plank, then lost his hide.
In "great sentimentality"…
The plank, "Broadwater," let it be.*

It hurt me that my father took Broadwater out of the realm of sentiment into the world of reality. It was just a stepping-stone from a war-ravaged homeland to what was to be a better and more peaceful future. It had served its purpose. I have since realized many bridges in life are just that—bridges.

As events turned out, my parent's homestead eventually became part of a new provincial park to protect ungulates.

Over the years it has witnessed many stages of disintegration and we have photos of the process. Even today it is only accessible by boat or some strong vehicle—preferably a four-wheel drive. Our grown-up children have both, on separate occasions, been able to find the remains. Celena brought me a beautiful bouquet of wild flowers that she collected from the wilderness meadow there. It is on display here at home—protected by cellophane. And Eric managed to haul out the wooden plank door that was once the entrance to the root house. It is now an important feature of our nature garden.

One afternoon, when we were living on Townsend Place, I discovered a recipe for red cabbage in the French Escoffier cookbook. One of the ingredients required Russet apples which we had growing on an ancient tree in our yard left over from the pioneer days. The frost had turned the apples sweet. Wind, rain and woodpeckers had knocked many to the ground. The children and I dressed warmly and went outside. Our long shadows and those from the swing hanging from one of the trees mingled with our laughter as we picked up the apples from among the pungent leaves. We put them in a basket and carried them up the back stairs into the kitchen.

I reached up to the shelf where I had stored the earthenware crock. It was exactly what the recipe called for. It was heavy. What a weight it must have been for my father to carry on his first visit! It was just like new, or I should say, just like when my father first handed it to me.

I peeled and cut up the apples, serving many

slices to the children. I layered the red cabbage, apples, butter and seasonings into the crock. The aroma from the oven reminded me of my mother's recipe.

Well, all this happened years ago. In my mind's eye I can still remember being on the farm and picking raspberries with my mother. We are singing *You are My Sunshine, I'll Take You Home Again Kathleen, Old Black Joe* and *Clementine* in two-part harmony. My mother, as I said before, was a fantastic alto.

Nearby, the weeping willow tree and that special swing are waiting, inviting me to come over and play.

Northern Song

"So, Mom, did you bring that sheet music you were raving about?" My daughter, son and I were just sitting down to have brunch at one of those charming Kitsilano restaurants.

I smiled and pulled it out of my bag. "It's a piece I just love but the chords are so difficult I can hardly get past the first few bars. The sound just sends me, so powerful. It's by Schumann."

"Hmm, "Northern Song" Eric said, looking down at the music. "The chords go in opposite directions."

"Really? No wonder I have trouble with it. Maybe you could learn it, dear. Even when you hear the first bar, you'll love the sound. It reminds me of your grandfather."

"Your dad, you mean."

"Yes, my dad. He was on the North Sea during the First World War."

Eric looked up. "I just read an article the other day about the North Sea. It's supposed to be one of the most turbulent waters in the world. Lots of shipwrecks, going back centuries. There's a virtual graveyard of ships down there. There was some effort to bring them up. But nobody's allowed permission. The Hood is there too. It was one of Britain's best but got sunk by the Bismark. Think it happened near Denmark. In just a couple of minutes a thousand lives were lost."

"I think that was the Second World War. Your grandfather was in the First."

"I heard a recent study," Eric continued. "They found out that the steel used in the Hood was the same as in the Titanic. I think it was in the same article. The steel was too brittle. No give."

Celena shook her head in disbelief. "Someone should have known not to use the same steel. There must have been some behind the scenes cover up."

Eric shrugged. "Maybe. Anyway the Hood just split apart, the bolts snapped. They had no give, no give at all. Just one blast did it. People at the time thought it must have been hit more than once to go down so fast, but it was just one and it went down with all those men...."

"By the way," I said, trying to change to a lighter subject, "did you know the name of the ship your grandfather was on?"

Celena and Eric shook their heads.

"Well, at the end of the First World War all German ships were ordered to Scapa Flow. You've heard of that, I'm sure. It's in Scotland."

They nodded.

"When your grandfather found out that his ship and all the German ships were going to be scuttled he took the first chance there was for repatriation. Remember the name of his ship? I think I told you before."

"Let me see," Eric said, "It must have been the HMS...."

"What?" I was shocked before I saw the twinkle in his eyes and laughed. "I don't think the name of a German ship would start with In His Majesty's...."

"No, hardly, Mom."

"But it could have been the Island Princess!" Celena offered. "You know the boat we took a cruise on?"

I shook my head.

"Then I have it!" Celena put up her hand excitedly. "It must have been the Love Boat!"

We all laughed.

I realized, however, that as successful as my children had become in their respective careers (and in their sense of humour) they certainly could use more knowledge about my father's life. Our order had not come yet. I had a captive audience. "Look," I said and took a deep breath. "Before I tell you the name of his ship, I'm going to explain something. The ship on which an admiral stays when he visits his fleet it called the flagship. Your grandfather was signaler on that ship. It was quite an honour."

"Mom, just give us a clue, just one letter." Celena said. "Just one letter."

Eric raised his index finger. "Just one word."

I ignored their appeals. "It was quite an honour. He said once during the war there was a big party on board and most of the crew were drunk. That's what he said. There were even women on board. He was on lookout and spotted a torpedo coming. He just had time to give the warning so his ship could turn. It was a narrow miss. Otherwise over 1000 crew would have been lost. He even got an award so he could attend a university."

"Which one?"

"Munich, a university in Munich," I answered. "So when he was selected for Frederick the Great...."

"Frederick the Great! Ah, you told us!" Celena and Eric laughed in unison. "Frederick the Great! We would have got it! Really, Mom, we would have remembered!"

"Oh, sure. What you two need is a history lesson, a history lesson about your heritage. Yes," I said, "that ship was named after the famous German king, King ...."

"So when you hear those chords," Eric interjected, "you think of your dad on the North Sea?"

"Yes, and in one of his letters to mom, before they got married, he gave his location as being 'on the billowing waves'. In German the words were 'auf Meereswogon'. Isn't that beautiful? So poetic!"

They glanced at each other.

I explained. "Of course he wasn't allowed to give his exact location. When he wrote that his ship was on training manoeuvres on the North Sea."

"Oh, there's the waiter!" Celena and Eric said almost in unison.

"Anyway, the opening chords of "Northern

Song" remind me of my father up in the crows nest, watching the horizon and hearing the rolling waves."

Celena reached for a bun. "That was very nice, Mom. Is the lesson over?"

Eric already had a bun on his plate. "Very interesting, Mom," he said, reaching for the butter.

Down by Stoney Creek

Eric was chopping up some branches in our back yard down by Stoney Creek. I was gardening nearby. Suddenly there was the sound of laughing, a whirring in the air and something hitting the bushes around us. Children from the elementary school across the ravine had decided to frighten us by throwing stones.

This was not the first time those children had made a nuisance of themselves: sliding down the steep slope, breaking branches and throwing litter around. The earth in the understory of the old growth forest had been so compacted with all

101

the traffic that virtually nothing would grow now. When I talked to the principal he said he had more pressing problems. The only solution, I had said hopefully (and repeatedly) seemed to be a chain link fence. That would help.

Several years of anticipation had come and gone. Perhaps I didn't explain myself clearly enough to the administration. Finding children in your back yard during recess and noon hour pulling up the stepping stones etc., was not that serious a problem to them. The school board could not afford the expense. (These were the days before the destruction of a riparian area was not considered important.) For whatever reason, nothing changed. The problem persisted.

But now this was the limit. "I'm going up to the house and phone the school," I shouted as I started up our pathway.

The line was always busy. I finally gave up and walked back down. I saw Eric, axe in hand, coming across the creek. No children anywhere!

"Where were you? What happened?"

"Been at the school," Eric laughed. "When the playground supervisor saw me coming, she called the children back up to the playground and herded them into the school. But I just followed them. Marched right in. Didn't even wipe the mud off my boots, just walked into the office. Laid my axe on the counter and explained the problem to the principal. He promised me the situation would be looked after."

About a week later there were hammering sounds coming from the direction of our back yard. When I went out to look, a six-foot high chain link fence was being erected on the boundary between the schoolyard and our ravine.

This spring I crossed the creek to see how nature was doing. Moss, ferns and even the trilliums were coming back to life. Now this riparian area is part of *The Oakdale Protected Habitat,* with a sign there to prove it.

A Little Episode

We were sitting at the breakfast table having our last cup of coffee on June 22, 2000. Walter was talking about his recent trip back to Germany for the 24th reunion of his engineering class. I had been reading one of his classmate's autobiographies.

"Well, what do you think of Artur's writing?" Walter asked.

"The writing is good. It seems, that as a child he was quite enamoured with Hitler."

"Well," Walter said, "Artur was even younger than me and couldn't have known better. There was a lot of enthusiasm for Hitler. I remember once when I had to stay in a special home. I was just eight years old."

"A special home?"

"Across the river, across the Elbe. My mother had to go in the hospital for an operation and the government arranged a place where children could stay while their mothers recovered. Anyway, the other children had already been at the place for awhile and knew each other. I had just arrived. Somehow the conversation came up about Hitler. I made a disparaging remark about him. The other children were shocked and I was sort of ostracized for the rest of the time—and I had to stay another six weeks. I was only eight years old. But I didn't care. Those kids didn't mean anything to me. I was homesick and in no mood to make friends anyway."

"Exactly what was your remark?"

"Ah, just some childish remark."

"What did you say?"

"It was just sort of silly and didn't make much sense. I remember but I really don't want to repeat it. Just a good thing it wasn't five years later. I could have been in big trouble."

"But that must have been before Hitler was even in power."

"Well, the Weimar Republic was trying to hang on to power but Hitler got elected January 30 of

1933. There were already policies in effect to round up communist enthusiasts or other dissidents."

"Where do you think the other boys got their ideas? From their parents?"

"Well, not necessarily. Those boys were all in the Pathfinders, sort of like the Boy Scouts here. The communists didn't have any uniforms but the Pathfinders had nice ones and had a lot of fun with so many things organized for young people to do. When Hitler got elected the uniforms changed a little. The shorts stayed black and there was still the triangular scarf around the neck with a leather ring to keep it on. All the knee socks were hand knit in those days. But the green shirts were changed to brown."

Brown shirts? That sounded familiar. "And where," I asked, "did you get the idea to be against Hitler at that early age?"

"My father was opposed to Hitler but," Walter added emphatically, "he wasn't a Communist either. In fact, one day, when my father was driving home in his carriage, some communists stopped him on the road and roughed him up a bit.

My stepbrother Erich, on the other hand, was twelve years older and he belonged to the

Communist Youth Organization. He heard the rumour that he was going to be picked up by some of Hitler's men so he joined the army. The army was still under Hindenberg, not under the control of the Nazi Party. Erich signing up for the army showed his loyalty to his country and that probably saved his life. That," Walter sighed, "is the way it was."

Later in the day, I thought about how our conversation at breakfast gave a glimpse into everyday life in the thirties—in Germany. I decided to write the event down and after dinner I showed Walter what I had recorded.

"Yes," he said, "that's the way it was. And about Erich, he had a 22-caliber rifle and got the bright idea of target practicing in the house so the shots couldn't be heard outside. Our house was quite large and had thick brick walls. He made a wood target and hung it on the door at the end of the upstairs hallway but he missed once and a bullet went into the doorframe. You can see the bullet hole today."And how did your mother feel about that?" I asked indignantly.

"My mother? Oh, she was sure angry. Erich didn't do it anymore. But that's the way the war affected the common people, the lower echelon, you might say."

"Unbelievable." I shook my head. "And that was over seventy years ago."

"Yes, you would have had to live during those times to understand."

"Walter? You know that episode, when you were a staying at that home? That must have been very uncomfortable for you, when the others ostracized you. How did you feel? Did you ever apologize to the other boys to get in their good favor again? Or say you really didn't mean what you said?"

"No," he said firmly.

Gold in the Cellar

The grapevine has to go. I entered my Gardener's Journal, November 1, 1997 "I hope the saw is sharp because you'll need it," I said to my husband. "The trunk is very thick."

He shrugged. "Ha! I'll just chop it off with my axe and cut it into pieces for firewood. It's just a nuisance, attracting all those raccoons. But it's your decision."

"No, take it down. It has to go."

This was not the first time the subject had come up. In recent years it took me two days of pruning to get the grapevine ready for winter. The side facing east was all tangled up in the wisteria vine. The other side had woven itself into our woodpile. On the side facing south, it trailed over the neighbour's hedge. Only the use of a rake and ladder could drag the vines back into our yard. I had to stand on the wooden carport railing to reach some of them and that two-by-four was almost thirty years old now. One day it could break. My doctor would shake her head and say, "You're paying a fine price for a few grapes. That fracture will take a while to heal."

I would miss the wreaths I made from the runners but making them was time consuming and now you can buy them in the stores for next to nothing. Not made in Canada of course. And it is almost impossible to find bundles of grapevines cut into lengths for kindling as I do with the extra pieces.

Lately the chilly night winds had scattered the old leaves, now feeling like scraps of tanned leather, along the driveway. What a mess to rake up. And they were in every corner of the flowerbeds. Who cares anyway? Is anybody going to miss that vine? Will the neighbours notice?

Our daughter might say, "Oh, it was so nice picking grapes from the kitchen sundeck. A feeling of bountifulness, fruit of the earth and all that." But she hasn't done that in years, being far too busy.

When I mentioned the plan to our son he said something about the raccoons having to eat and we have to give something back to nature. I was surprised when he added, "And isn't that grape vine part of our heritage? Weren't there some memories?"

Yes, there were memories. That grapevine, or its ancestor I should say, was growing on the little dairy farm my parents bought when they arrived in the Fraser Valley in 1929. They propagated the grapevine and made a sturdy arbor from which they suspended a small canvas jumper swing for me. They painted what was once a chicken house blue and white, calcimined the interior and made it into a cozy home. When my parents moved to a fifty-five acre dairy farm in East Chilliwack, they took along enough grape roots to plant a row screening the bee hives from the road. As a little girl I remember lying under the trailing vines on warm September days and having a wonderful feed just a reach away.

Years later when I married and my husband and I built our new home my dad brought me a root. I had asked for it. We planted it on south side of our house next to the cement foundation. He said— or maybe it was my mother—that the roots love being next to cement. That vine grew and grew.

The first year it reached the railing on the side of the carport, the second year my husband put up a wire for it to climb along. Then it reached for the upstairs deck off our kitchen where it ranked both east and west. The huge leaves protected the ripening grapes and shaded the carport too. It was like southern France or Italy. And even on hot summer days the sundeck was very enjoyable. We called it "Patio Paradise".

In the spring I picked the young, tender leaves for making dolmades and gave some to friends who enjoy making this Greek delicacy.

When the grapes ripen they smell like honey. They were not purple or red. They were not seedless. They were green. But the flavour—if you knew how to eat them! You just squish them between your teeth, letting the sweet juice fill your mouth and then swallow them whole.

The trouble is that in recent years the raccoons discovered them. They could smell them too. Just when I got my first taste and said to myself, "Hmm. A little green yet, give them a few more days," then the raccoons would come up our back stairs from the ravine below. They didn't like the skins and spit them out all over the deck. And marks from their muddy paws were all over our white stucco every day. I tried discouraging them by spraying ammonia around and covering them with chicken wire but that didn't work.

This year, after the raccoon's first party, I decided to pick the crop, ripe or not. That was a wonderful sunny day. I harvested almost ten pounds. I made grape jelly with added sugar and honey to take the place of missed sunshine. It turned out to be even better than gooseberry jam. We love it on buttered toast for breakfast. It makes a delicious milkshake and is absolutely mouth watering on pancakes.

When I visit our cellar, those golden green jars of grape jelly make a fine contrast to the glow of red cherries, yellow apricots and purple plums.

Of course, the grape vine is now gone.

Jingi

When I was growing up on our dairy farm in East Chilliwack, I had a cat. She was the smartest cat in the world. My dad said she was the best hunter of mice we ever had. One day he told me to come to the implement shed; he wanted to show me something. I was holding her in my arms when he opened the box on the seed spreader. As soon as he lifted the lid, I could see mice scampering in every direction. My cat bolted out of my arms and in a few lightening movements she had one mouse under each of her four paws and two in her mouth. That's how smart she was.

Of course, any cat, however intelligent, can use a helping hand at times. So occasionally I would go out into the field and dig up mouse holes just so she wouldn't have to wait so long. In the summer I brought saucers of milk to her nest in the hay so she could teach her hungry kittens to drink. I loved snuffling my nose into the clean, milky smell of their roly poly tummies. Once, when my parents though I was lost, they found me fast asleep—with her kittens curled up in my lap. I was just kitten sitting while their mother was out hunting.

Often, I tried to teach my cat things that would enrich her life in one way or another. I wanted her to ride with me on that special swing my father had built me, the one that hung from our old weeping willow tree, but she didn't like that, even when I wrapped her up like a baby.

Once, when she was watching me catch minnows with a tin can in the little ditch in front of our farm, I decided to teach her how to swim. She might find this skill handy one day. Each time I put her in the water she hopped out and shook herself off getting me all wet in the process.

In winter I tried to teach her to follow paths between walls of snow I had built just for her but she managed to jump out. Every time I picked her up to give her more practice she looked at me—a little sadly I thought—and scrambled out again.

One warm day my friend, Gail, and I were sitting on the front steps of our farmhouse, next to a big rhododendron that was full of pinky white blossoms. We were using my cat to model some doll clothes.

Gail looked at my cat, now sprawled out on the grass, resting after having pawed off the doll's cap we had tied around her chin. "Your cat should have a name."

"She does have a name. It's Kitty."

"That's not a name. I mean a real name."

"I know that," I quickly replied, "but no name is good enough. If she were all white we could call her Snowball or Snowy. But she's got so many colours: black, brown and grey, white and even orange. If she were all white it would be easy."

"Think of something you like a lot and call her that."

I thought for a moment. "Well, I like Christmas. Christmas is my favourite thing."

Gail shook her head.

"But I don't think I could call her 'Christmas'," I said taking the cue.

"No," Gail added solemnly, "no, that name is too long and I don't think it's right to call a cat Christmas."

"I know," I said. "But it could be something to do with Christmas. Oh," I said, "talking about Christmas makes me wish it were Christmas right now!" And I started to clap my hands and sing:

Jingle bells, jingle bells,
Jingle all the way.
Oh what fun it is to ride."

"You can't sing that," Gail interrupted sticking her hands in the pockets of her overalls. "It's summer. You can't sing a Christmas song in summer! It's not right."

"Oh yeah, I can too, " I said, hooking my thumbs in the straps of my overalls. "A good song is a good song all year long and it's so favourite I think I'll call my cat Jingle. No, that too Christmassy. I'll call her Jingi. Then every time I call her, I'll think of Jingle Bells but nobody will know. And when I think of Jingle Bells, I'll think of Christmas and Christmas is my favourite thing and I started singing:

Jingi plays, Jingi plays
Jingi plays all day.
Jingi is my favourite cat
And that's the way she'll stay.

From that day on I called my cat Jingi and when I said Jingi I thought of Jingle Bells and when I thought of Jingle Bells, I thought of....

One day my mother and I got a ride with the milk truck into Vancouver. She wanted to buy a bedroom suite with the money she had earned from picking hops. When we came home the next day, Jingi didn't come running to greet me.

I looked at Dad. "Where's Jingi?"

"I'll show you. She's in the barn."

I followed him to the area where the cows were milked, where Jingi would often be found taking a nap on the undulating belly of a cow that was lying down in the straw. I saw Jingi stretched out on a wide board. I ran over to her but she didn't move.

"She's dead," Dad said in a low voice.

"How? How come?" I tried to lift her up. I looked at Dad and then back again at Jingi.

"You know," my dad answered gravely, "she was thirteen years old. That's a pretty good age for a hard working farm cat." He lifted up her head and put his finger in her mouth to show me her gums. "See? She just had one tooth left. She could hardly eat anymore."

I had never thought of Jingi being old; I just took her for granted. I knew she was about my age but I wasn't even quite a teenager yet. Later I found out that a cat's first two years are counted as twenty-five human years and each year after is counted as four human years so Jingi would have been about seventy years old.

Mom gave me a piece of black tar paper in which to wrap her. I sprinkled purple clover, dandelions, white daisies and buttercups all around her. I knew she liked these flowers; I had used them for making her necklaces. But first I got my mother's scissors and cut souvenir samples of hair from different parts of her body: white, black, brown, grey and orange. I wrapped them in wax paper and put the package in an old cigar box. Then I dug a hole under the pinky white rhododendron at the foot of our farmhouse steps. I buried her there next to the place where Jingi was given her name.

Ruby Earrings

"That was Celena on the phone," I shouted to my husband. "She said hi."

"What did she want?"

I knew what our daughter wanted to discuss with her father but said casually, "Oh, nothing. Nothing really." But then I added, "But she has a little problem she wants to talk to you about."

"A problem? What is it?"

"She said she'd call you."

"Tell me what it is." A cloud passed over his features. "Tell me now."

"No, she'll call. You can discuss it with her then."

"Come on dear, tell me." His blue eyes were as warm as a summer sky.

"Tell me now."

I hesitated. "Promise you won't get upset?"
"Sure, I promise, " he answered, a little too quickly,
I thought.

"Well...." I took a deep breath. "She doesn't like
the earrings you gave her for Christmas."

"What?" His eyes turned into bolts of lightning.
"You're fooling!"

"I love the ones you gave me," I said, trying
to smooth over the situation with a placating
response. "And she loves them too but she says
hers are...well, she says you gave her a similar pair
a few years ago and they're just beautiful. They
have a wonderful design. She wears them all the
time. She doesn't need another pair with rubies.
Just plain ones would be nice, something she can
wear with almost anything would be better. Don't
take it personally...".

"I can't believe it," he interjected. "Well, that's it.
I'll never get that girl anything again."

"Oh, you always say that."

"I suppose she'd like the rubies taken out and
replaced with diamonds? Ha, ha. Do you know
how much diamonds that big would cost?"

"No, no. That wouldn't be necessary. Just plain

gold is great. Maybe with a little diamond. But the ruby.... Well, it doesn't go with some outfits."

"Do you know how much I paid for those things?"

"Lots. Probably close to $500.00," I ventured. He had expensive tastes, especially when it came to jewelry.

"Yours cost even more."

"I love mine; they match my necklace. Celena likes my earrings, too, but she's not that happy with hers. She needs earrings but would rather have other ones for work."

"She seemed happy when I gave them to her."

"She didn't want to hurt your feelings at Christmas when she got them. I only found out how she felt about them a few weeks ago."

"Christmas was only a few weeks ago."

"Well, I meant a couple of weeks ago. I guess time flies. I thought she liked them too, when she got them.... But then she told me they looked like earrings for an old lady."

"Well, then they're just right for her. She's almost thirty!"

"Well, I like them. You can give her cash and maybe give them to me for Valentine's."

"Ha! And spend that much money? Do you know

how much yours cost? $800.00! And that was a special price!'

"Well, I love mine," I repeated once again. "The way they close with a hinge and how they go exactly with my necklace. Celena likes mine too."

"Well, when she phones I'll tell her that's the last time I'm giving her anything! Remember that brown coat I got her when she was thirteen? She wouldn't wear it. She would not wear it! I brought it all the way from Europe and she just put it on once and then left it in the closet."

"I wouldn't bring all that up again. I shouldn't have told you why she called. Now, I've just made trouble by telling you."

"No, no. You did the right thing. Telling me gives me time to cool down. Gives me a warning. If she phoned and just said that...." His voice trailed off. "I'd have said...." He hesitated. "Now I have a warning."

"That's good. Otherwise, I'd be sorry I told you."

"You know what I thought when you said she had a problem?" My husband's voice softened. "I thought she had an accident with her car or maybe she bumped into someone, not bad, but anyway.... Or maybe she didn't get that promotion she was after. Maybe they just fired her instead."

"Well," I smiled broadly. "In comparison, this is really nothing, right? If you had the receipt she could just return them for something she likes, something she can wear with more things."

"Well, I think I got it alright but I can't remember if I put it on Visa or paid cash."

"Even the Visa bill would do," I said, relieved about his change of tone.

"You know," my husband's voice interjected, "those earrings are beautiful. When she calls I'm going to tell her that she's a spoilt brat, absolutely spoilt, not liking expensive earrings with rubies. Everyone at the store loved them!"

"Well, dear, Celena doesn't like them. She just didn't want to spoil your Christmas."

"Well, when she phones I'm really going to give it to her."

"Oh, for heaven's sake, don't do that. I told her I thought this would be a good night to talk to you. Anyway Randy doesn't like them either. He says they look like they belong to an old lady."

"Randy? That boyfriend? He's a real troublemaker. He's the one who's always pushing her to get that promotion. What's he going to be like if they get married if he's already behind the scenes manipulating."

"Look, dear, when Celena calls just say, 'Darling, I'm so glad you are being frank and open with me. You should never hesitate. We can always consult about these things.'"

"Ha, ha!" my husband said sarcastically.

"Sure," I continued, ignoring the tone of his voice, "you can say, 'Of course you can have the receipt and get something that makes you happy.'"

"Hm. I'm going to bring up the brown coat."

"Oh, for heaven's sake, don't do that. Now I'm sorry you squeezed it out of me."

"No, you did the right thing. As husband and wife shouldn't we be honest with each other?"

I nodded weakly. "Then just say, 'Celena, I'm so glad you are being frank with me. Of course, you can return it. You could have told me before. Anytime you want to talk....'"

The phone rang. We both looked at it. My husband reaches for the receiver. "Hi, Celena. He beckons me to come closer. "What's up?"

"Everything's great," I hear her say.

"Nothing new?"

"Well.... I'm just thinking of those beautiful

earrings you gave me for Christmas."

"Aha! You like them! You haven't lost them?"

"No, Dad, no. But you know.... they're a lot like another pair you got for me a few years ago."

"Really? I can't remember. You'll have to show me. Come over and show me."

"Okay. Oh," her voice changes to a whisper, "I've got to go. Randy's at the door."

"What did she say?" I asked after he put down the receiver. "I couldn't hear everything."

"Just that she has two pairs of earrings almost the same. I told her she should show me. That's all we said. Randy was at the door."

"I can't believe it. She's worried stiff about the whole thing. I told her to discuss it with you and now she doesn't even admit that she wants to exchange them. I'm going to phone her."

"Yes, you phone her. Tell her I have the receipt. Tell her she can do whatever she wants. It's up to her. It's okay. She doesn't need to worry. She has enough on her mind."

Erna Mattson

Erna was an elderly lady whom our family befriended when she moved into Coquitlam. She was gracious, kind and generous and though suffering from various ailments she always dressed with such care and style that it made you happy just to look at her.

When I visited to socialize or do errands, she often shared reminiscences and anecdotes that opened up other worlds and eras. Some stories were humorous and others were sad, but all were interesting. She had an amazing memory and never repeated herself unless requested to do so.

She talked about her advantaged youth in Sweden. Once a year her family served a crêpe breakfast under the trees on their estate. It was a festival to which the young and old, the rich and poor from the entire community were invited.

As a young woman she contracted tuberculosis. Her husband to be waited several years until she was well enough to marry.

Erna told of the day when she and some other married friends were visiting May Maxwell in her home in Montreal. May's husband was the famous Canadian architect, William Sutherland Maxwell. The women were having tea in the drawing room. Their discussion was about the Baha'i Faith and some charitable works in which they were involved. Suddenly, Mr. Maxwell appeared at the doorway with an armful of socks and said, "It is all very well that you are so enjoying yourselves with spiritual matters but I can't find one pair of socks that doesn't have a hole." He placed the socks on a table and left the room. When he looked in shortly after all the women were busy mending his socks—and still having a good time.

One day I asked her about the small metal bowl that was always on her antique sewing table. As usual, it was a fascinating story and I asked her to write it down. Here is her story as written. She called it Pandora's Box and dated it 1982.

My husband and I lived in Simla, Punjab, India where he was stationed at the time, working on a hydroelectric project for the government. The year was 1947, early in September. The independence of India had taken place on August 15 of that year. Soon afterwards the partition of the country was announced. It meant Hindustan for the Hindus, Pakistan for the Muslims. And riots broke out all over the country. Pakistan persecuted the Sikhs and Hindus, Hindustan the Muslims. Law and order seemed no longer existent. The British were leaving India.

We had Muslim servants: the cook, head bearer, gardener and their small families. Their quarters, called "Godowas" were beneath our own flat.

The riots broke out in the big cities but finally reached Simla. They soon reached out little sanctuary in the mountains.

All Muslim shops were burned and ransacked, rickshaw coolies killed and their rickshaws broken. We lost three of our boys because they did not live on our compound. Soon Sikhs who had been dispossessed of their homes and killed, lower down in the mountains came up to Simla to take revenge on any Muslim they could get their hands on. Our servants were in constant danger. We protected them the best we could by hiding them in one room upstairs during the night. This room could be reached only by getting through our own bedroom. My husband slept with a revolver on the night table for about ten days. Then we were warned by one of our engineers, a Sikh, that our house would be attacked the following day and our own life would be in danger as well.

We spent a sleepless night praying and making plans. With the help of the British officer who had supplied the weapon and ammunition, we were allowed to take our servants, including their friends and relatives, during the 2 to 4 p.m. curfew to the safety of Royal Lodge two miles away. It would go too far to describe this weary long trek on a narrow mountain road with twenty-three terrified men, women and children. But we arrived safely and the poor people remained at the "Godowas" at the Royal Lodge until armed transport could be arranged to take them to refugee camps from where they would be taken to Karachi in Pakistan.

The day before the train was to leave we visited our servants once more. Mohamed, our head bearer and his family came to kneel in front of us, with his forehead on the ground and held out to me the shabby little brass bowl my eyes still rested on. It was the most precious of his meager possessions. It had been in his mother's family for generations. It was only used on Muslim holidays, like Ramadan to hold small coins or sweets for anyone who called at their home.

I did not want to accept the gift that had meant so much to him and his family. But I also could not refuse it and hurt his pride and his wish to thank us for saving his and the life of his family. We took a sad farewell.

The bowl will mean nothing to anyone but me. My friends made fun of me many times for keeping it in open view with real nice objects that one collects during the years. It is old and shabby but has the classic form of even the simplest objects in daily use by poor

*people in the Far East. It is always a delight
to behold. And of course this little bowl is full
of secrets and memories.*

She didn't mention seeing an entire truck full
of men, each with one hand chopped off, being
driven out of their area. I guess it was just too
gruesome to put down in writing.

Novels such as *A Fine Balance* by Rohinton
Mistry reinforces the tragedy of this period of
India's history and makes it very understandable.

Erna explained that when her husband accepted
the position in India they had to put their son in
a boarding school in Switzerland. She took great
efforts to find the best school for her son and he
seemed happy. He overcame a weight problem from
which he had suffered since a childhood illness. He
was very successful in his studies. However, one
day when he had just started university and was
not yet twenty he wrote that he wished to marry.
Erna immediately set off for Switzerland. Though
his girlfriend—the first he had ever had—was very
pretty, she felt (and apparently voiced this feeling)
that he was too young to make such a serious
decision. This angered the young couple and led

to an estrangement with Erna, which lasted even after the couple married.

This situation had existed for about twenty years at the time I met Erna. When she told me about the estrangement and how it saddened her, it saddened me too. I asked her what I could do and she finally consented for me to write them and arrange to visit them in Norway on my next trip to Europe. Though her son and his wife were very hospitable, nothing I said caused them to change their attitude. As usual the annual Christmas card arrived with its few impersonal words. Even though her son had become an atomic scientist of some renown, giving lectures around the world, he never visited his mother.

Erna and I shared many experiences. Once, when my husband was out of town, I spent the night in her apartment as she had just been in the hospital because of angina attacks. She was home with instructions to rest, move slowly and not let anything excite her. I spent an uneasy night on the sofa, as I was worried that she might have an attack and then what would I do? Nursing was not one of my strengths. I was happy to see the first glimmerings of dawn through the curtains as

I knew a homemaker would be soon be arriving to help her with her morning routine.

Suddenly the shrill blare of a fire alarm pierced the building's early morning silence. I couldn't believe it. Surely it was a mistake. Someone would shut it off. But the sound persisted. I quickly dressed and looked out into the hallway only to see the faces of other concerned residents doing the same. Erna, who was hard of hearing, called from her bedroom. "What is it? What is that noise?"

"Oh, it's nothing. But you might as well get up since you're awake." She looked at me quizzically but cooperated. Slowly, ever so slowly, I helped her get out of bed. And carefully I helped her into her dressing gown. Finally, Erna was in her wheelchair.

Through my mind went wild scenarios. Keep calm! The local newspaper will have headlines.... Friend escapes. Elderly lady collapses as fire rages through building.... Friend escapes. Keep calm.

"What is going on?" she kept asking. "Why are we going out into the hallway?"

And I was thinking, when will she have her next attack?

Suddenly the air was pierced by noiselessness.

The alarm was off! A neighbour came running down the corridor announcing that it had been a false alarm. I sighed inwardly (as Erna probably did as well), turned the wheelchair around and pushed her back into her apartment. That was the first and last time I ever spent an entire night with Erna. I think we both agreed that it was a terrible experience.

When Erna died, I buried her ashes under some giant redwoods in Como Lake Park. The trees had been planted just the previous year and she had been very happy about it, as she knew Sir Richard St. Barbe Baker in whose honor they were planted. The brass plaque is inscribed:

REDWOODS

These trees are dedicated in memory of
Richard St. Barbe Baker (1889-1992)
Forester, Author, Conservationist
Donated by the Baha'i Youth of
Coquitlam
March 21, 1985

Irma loved nature but she also loved people. There, in the most popular park in Coquitlam, she would have both. Those redwoods have really grown. Their strength and grace always remind me of her. I wish her son would come to see them, even now. I did send a letter describing the location.

Erna gave me some of her belongings as I helped her move from her large apartment to a nursing home, from one nursing home to another and then finally a hospital. The pewter wall sconce in our kitchen is from her Swedish heritage as is the burgundy and green weaving which is often on our dining room table during the winter months. The antique Meissen inkwell adorned with two children reading a book is from Erna as is her brass seal she once used with sealing wax. The small salt and pepper shakers made of cut glass, silver and mother of pearl are special, as they were once a gift to Erna from her son when he was still a young boy. The ornamental fish crafted from pine and wrought iron is now used to protect our table from hot dishes just as it once protected her table. The deep brown and gold sari was a parting gift from her husband's company when they finally left India. I have worn it at a multicultural event. The bookcase in our den with the glass and wrought iron doors is something she picked up in a second hand store. There also the copper burner, which holds two candles, so handy for keeping tea warm. Thinking of tea, she also gave me a beautiful rose and gold mug, which had been in her family for generations. The pretty multicoloured tin container, made in England, is used in my kitchen—as it was in hers—for tea leaves.

In the kitchen also are many plates and platters on which are painted in oriental design delft blue parakeets with tropical flowers. These dishes are very old and come from the captain's table of a whaling ship. Erna told me that the factory in Gustafsberg, Sweden, reran this pattern called "Nankin" early in the twentieth century for those collectors who were missing pieces. She said a relative had found a box of this newer edition in their cellar. It had been stored there unused for over fifty years.

Not to be omitted is the exquisite oil painting of Ragnar, her husband, painted when he was still a child in 1895. The frame is much older. The large black and white antique print on strips of parchment is also from India. She presented this piece of art when she joined us at one of our Christmas dinners. On the frame backing is attached an envelope. In it there is an explanation in her own handwriting of what the print depicts: *Ganesh, the Elephant God, doing "war against ignorance, which causes most of the evil in the world."*

An old walnut ashtray stand in our living room holds a bouquet of miniature porcelain flowers. You may notice that the daisies match those in the painting on the wall above

And the stand matches the lamp beside the piano in both design and finish. What is easily overlooked is the little metal bowl, which holds the flowers.

Tammy

Somebody tugged at my sleeve. A voice whispered anxiously, "Liberian, liberian, they're fightin' at the back of the libery."

I looked up and spotted two hefty adolescents, partly screened by a bookshelf at the back of the library. I was determined that the first morning in my very own library was not going to be ruined by a couple of roughnecks. I walked over to them. They were breathing heavily and snorting obscenities, glaring at each other like two stags locked in combat. "Boys! Boys, stop fighting!" I shouted. They didn't seem to hear me.... "Put your fists down, boys." Their legs traded lightning kicks as I tried to step between them. I looked around.

Mr. Kenkel, the principal, was approaching with long, determined steps. "At it again, I see," he said, putting a hand on each of their shoulders. He dismissed me with a passing nod as he marched them out into the hallway.

As the sound of their footsteps going to the office gradually receded, I sat down again behind the circulation desk, thankful that it was loaded with piles of books. I concentrated on the rows of overdue book cards, trying to ignore the curious eyes of the others in the library.

"Liberian? You know what?" It was that same anxious voice. "Those boys fightin'...?"

A slim girl, perhaps nine or ten years old, was staring at me with dark eyes, twining a strand of her light brown hair around her fingers.

"Yes?" I nodded, hoping to give an appearance of calmness and efficiency, wondering what was going to happen next.

"The one with the big boots," she continued, "that was my brother, Brad."

I glanced towards the doorway through which the two boys had just been escorted. "I see," I said, trying to sound casual. "Does that happen here often?"

She squinted her eyes and hesitated as though the question puzzled her.

"Fighting, I mean, here in the library?"

"Mm....not too much," was her disquieting reply. "Brad... he... He jus' fights 'cause of that other guy. That guy keeps callin' me names."

She lingered and I continued working, anxious to choose the right words. I looked up at her again.

"What's your name?" I tried to change the subject away from her brother.

"Tammy."

"Tammy," I smiled approvingly. "That's a pretty name."

Her eyes widened. She gave an almost imperceptible smile but said nothing, trying to get the straggle of hair to stay behind her ear.

"Well, Tammy, I guess it feels good to have a brother who cares for you so much."

For a few moments she seemed to be thinking over what seemed to be an unfamiliar idea. She shifted from one foot to the other. "Yeah, I guess so," she finally said. The bell rang for the end of recess. "Maybe...?" She hesitated. "Maybe, could I help you in the libery? I helped at my last school. I did lots of things," she added with a worried but persistent voice. The strand of hair had fallen into her face again. She looked like only ten or eleven years old, at the most.

"Usually I only take grade six or sevens for monitors...."

"I'm in grade six," she interjected. "I'm twelve!"

"That would be great then," I responded. "Do you think you could come in at noon today?"

Her eyes lit up and she squared her small shoulders. Suddenly her slight body seemed to unfurl like a flag on a parade. "At lunch?"

I nodded. "Yes, right at 12:30 when the door opens."

Tammy skipped out into the hallway. Her knee socks sagged down around her puddle-colored shoes, her worn cotton dress danced beneath a tight, once pink sweater that was too small to be buttoned, but was.

From that morning on Tammy helped whenever she could, before school, at recess, lunch and after school, even sometimes during the day when her class work was finished. The cluttered grayness of the library underwent a metamorphosis. Tammy helped to rearrange the chairs and tables. Tammy tidied the stacks of brightly colored rug samples donated by the carpet store across the street that the kindergarten children used as pillows on the linoleum floor. A listening post was set up in one corner and beside it, against the wall; a chameleon lived in a leafy terrarium. Tammy always checked that it had flies and pieces of her apple to eat.

Colourful book jackets designed by the art class were stapled high above the fiction shelves. A Social Studies teacher supplied a long transportation mural made by her students for the wall over the non-fiction books. Kaleidoscopic butterfly posters, left over from a department store display, brightened the bulletin board next to the entrance. And some grade seven boys had proudly presented some relics, a bear's skull they found in the bush behind the school.

Through the window, the view of lopsided bicycle stands and the littered playground were now camouflaged by a lacy green curtain of rabbits foot and asparagus fern as well as cascading spider plants. Tammy faithfully tended them with our special watering can painted on one side with a wild rose.

The library was a warm and friendly center of activity but changing the physical environment of the library was easier than teaching the library curriculum that, among other things, included the proper care of books.

The neighbourhood was a haven for anyone in financial need. Its makeshift suites in deteriorating houses waiting to be torn down by developers had very low rents. Broken homes, substance abuse and unemployment were common. As well as the obvious physical needs made evident by the safety-pinned flies, stale odors and torn clothing, many of these children were virtually screaming out their need for love and security. A steady ebb and flow of children changed the school's enrollment almost every day.

One morning, Tammy put her hands on her hips and exclaimed with a self-satisfied sigh, "The only thing's the matter now in this here library," (for the first time she is no longer mispronouncing library) "is all these messy books. We should throw them all out and buy new ones." She caught my eye and continued. "See this one here?" She reached into the return box and pulled out a dinosaur book. "It's falling apart!" Tammy handed it to me and I looked at the torn cover and flipped through the finger-smudged pages. Somebody had marked a new caption in bright blue ink beside the plesiosaurus, and a red felt marker had changed the anatomy of a stegosaur.

"You won't be able to erase that," I sighed.

Tammy proceeded to pull out more books and push them across the circulation desk. "Look! Someone has cut pictures out of this encyclopedia! A dirty Kleenex! Someone has left their dirty Kleenex right in a library book! Ugh," she squeaked, dangling it in from of me. "These books should all be thrown into the garbage. Those kids should not be allowed to take books out if they're so careless."

"If we threw out all the dirty or damaged books," I laughed, "there wouldn't be any to sign out anyway."

"Yeah," she giggled, "they'd have to get them from the garbage dump and it would serve them right!"

"Well, not everyone is careless. You're a good example, Tammy. You don't damage books when you sign them out."

"Oh no!" Her brown eyes flashed as she shook her head. "I would never do that!" she said, adjusting her hair. I noticed that her wrists were covered with a thin, grey film, a common sight in this school. She wore a large black diamond on her middle finger. Her fingernails had traces of different shades of polish, pink, magenta, scarlet. I moved closer to her.

"That's a beautiful ring you're wearing," I said, taking her hand in mine.

"Yeah, my older sister gave it to me. She found it."

"It's very big," I said, examining it carefully. "Tammy, has anyone ever told you that you have beautifully shaped hands?"

She looked at her hands and shrugged.

"Tammy how would you like me to give you a manicure one day?"

She said nothing.

It crossed my mind that she might think it would cost money. "Free of charge," I added, "because you've been such a great help here."

"Man...man-a-koor?" She moved her lips carefully. "Is that," she hesitated, "is that when you make your nails all fancy?"

"That's about it. Do you want to give it a try?"

She shrugged. "Okay, why not?"

"It's a deal then," I said with an inward sigh of relief. "What about tomorrow at eight, when you first come in? I'll bring my manicure supplies."

Next morning Tammy was waiting at the library door. "Did you bring your stuff?"

"It's all right here, " I pointed to my briefcase. "This is going to be fun! I kept talking to her as we walked towards the workroom door. I filled the sink with warm water and added some fragrant bubble soap that I had brought in a little bottle. I rolled up her sleeves and Tammy put her hands (which had not noticeably changed from the day before) into the bubbles. She giggled. I gently brushed the dirt from under the fingernails of one hand and then the other. Polish remover, cotton balls, cuticle remover, clippers and a file all had their effect. I guided her hands into the warm water again and again, finally drying them with a soft yellow towel. Some little moons were showing and the hangnails were gone. I massaged her hands with lily-of-the-valley scented hand cream.

Tammy smelled her hands and looked at them admiringly. "I think I'll get my Mom to buy us one of those," she said, pointing to the nailbrush. "It sure does the trick." She looked at her hands and then at me. "Can we do this again? Someday?"

Suddenly, several voices piped up from the

audience that had formed at the workroom doorway. "Can I have one too?" "Can't we have turns?" "I'd like to try one too!"

Of course Brad had to slouch by at that moment, hands in pockets. "What's goin' on?" he snickered. "Manicures? Man oh man. That's a new one for the library!"

I tried to think of a quick comeback but he was gone again before I had a chance. "So is fighting," I should have said.

Anyway, from that time on, 8 a.m. manicures became a common occurrence in the library workroom. On parents day several mothers and fathers came in to express their appreciation. Mr. Kenkel approved.

One morning, Tammy didn't show up. The nine o'clock bell had already gone. Rain was spattering on the windowpanes. I was putting some books on the shelves, a routine task that Tammy usually did, when suddenly she came rushing in. "I can't help you today, I'm goin'!"

"What?" I exclaimed, taken aback, "Going where?"

"Leavin' the school," she said with a little shrug of her shoulders. "We're goin' to Alberta, to my Granny's. She's got a big house and I get to have my very own bedroom and my Dad promised he'd visit us sometimes 'cause he's got hired and he's got hisself a job!"

"Oh!" I said, putting my armful of books down on the circulation desk and smiling at her. "Well, that's wonderful! That's wonderful, Tammy. Good for you! You lucky girl!" I put on a bright face. "When are you leaving?"

"Tomorrow."

"Tomorrow?"

"Yeah, we have to be out by tomorrow.... I jus' came back to clean up my locker and...."

"Is Brad going too?"

"Yeah, he's goin' to get hisself a job too. I got to pack. I jus' came back to...."

"You're leaving now? Right now?"

She nodded.

"You..., I..." I was at a loss for words. "You've been such a great help."

"Yeah," Tammy answered, her eyes darted around the library.

I quickly walked over to the workroom sink and picked up the little watering can standing on the counter. "A little gift," I said, handing it to her. "A little gift for all your help."

"For me?" Her eyes lit up as her hands cradled it.

"Yes, just for you, Tammy. I hope you'll have room in your suitcase."

She touched the rose painted on one side and then held the watering can up to me. "Won't you need it?" she asked in almost a whisper, reaching it to me.

"No, no I have another one at home. Take it as a keepsake." I put it in a plastic book bag and handed it back.

Tammy clutched it to her chest, then suddenly turned and ran out the door.

There was a tug at my heart as I sat down behind the circulation desk. I had to get ready for the next class. I took a deep breath. It was raining harder now. I got up and looked out the window through the green curtain of ferns, past the bicycle stand and across the wet windswept grounds. A young girl came into view. Some plastic bags filled with who knows what were bouncing against her legs as she ran. It was Tammy.

The Little Wild Rose

Long ago, at the edge of a forest, a crow found a rose hip, the seed of a wild rose. He held it in his beak and flew to a country mailbox beside a farm road. "What a fine place to eat my snack!" he said.

The crow put the rose hip down, but it rolled into the tall grass and leaves below. The crow looked and looked but couldn't see it. Finally, he flew away.

The rose hip stayed hidden. Soon winter came, covering the seed with a blanket of snow. The cold winds did not disturb it. The wolves that ran across the moonlit fields did not disturb it. Even the mailman who opened and closed the squeaky

155

door of the country mailbox did not disturb the rose hip. The seed slept quietly all winter long.

When spring came, the sun and warm breezes melted away the snow. The little seed woke up. First one tiny root appeared, then another. Finally, small leaves poked out and a baby rose was born. What an exciting day! There was fresh air. There was sunshine. There were noises, too. The rose hip had heard sounds when she was under the ground, but now they were much louder.

At first the baby rose could hardly see anything because she was too small. She could only see stems holding up a dark leafy tent. Even the field mouse was bigger.

The baby rosebush grew more roots that reached for water and food in the soil below.

She sprouted more leaves that reached up to the sunshine. By summer she grew tall enough to peek over the grasses and watch butterflies and grasshoppers playing in a golden world of buttercups and dandelions.

Soon autumn and winter came again with its cold wind. Rabbits and deer left tracks in the snow around the sleeping rosebush.

Then one fine spring day, the rosebush grew tall

enough to see a ditch along the country road. A mother duck was teaching her ducklings how to dive for snacks among the reeds, swim in straight rows, and quack with each other. Overhead she heard hundreds of blackbirds sharing news while they sat on the telephone pole wires. She heard the swallows twittering to each other as they zigzagged across the sky.

The rosebush felt very lonely. "Everyone has somebody to talk to except me. I don't even have one friend! Nobody even knows I'm alive!"

Then one morning, a little girl started coming to stand beside the country mailbox. But after a few minutes a big yellow bus rumbled down the road and took her away. The rosebush always watched the little girl and tried to get her attention by stretching her branches to touch her but she wasn't close enough. Anyway, the little girl was too busy doing other things.

In the fall she scratched hopscotch lines on smooth parts of the gravel road or sang rhymes as she skipped with her yellow rope. In winter the little girl would sometimes break pieces of ice from the frozen puddles and place them on the mailbox. When the school bus brought her back home in the afternoon, the little girl would check to see if the ice had melted during the day. When spring came, the little girl picked buttercups and forget-me-nots from the side of the road. "I know that bouquet is not for me," the rosebush complained. "She doesn't even know that I'm here!"

But the rosebush was growing bigger and one morning the little girl looked straight at her. "How beautiful!" she exclaimed. "Pink roses are blooming right beside our mail-box!" She gently touched a soft petal and a drop of morning dew rolled onto the little girl's fingertip. Then she smelled the sweet perfume.

After that day the little girl would say kind words to the wild rose. "How are you today?" she would say or "My, you're beautiful! I think another bud is coming!" In dry weather she would say, "Are you thirsty, dear rose?" and then she sprinkled the rosebush with water from her watering can. The rosebush was so happy to have a friend.

One day when the little girl visited she touched the rose bush gently and whispered, "You are my favorite flower in the whole world but.... But, our family is moving away to the city. I have come to say good-bye."

When the girl walked away across the road, the

rosebush cried. "Oh dear, I thought I had a friend forever! How could she leave, just like that? I feel I have always known that sweet girl. I will never forget her smile, her laugh and her gentle touch as long as I live. I will never forget her, even if she forgets me."

The rosebush looked at the autumn colours around her country home. She looked at her own pink roses that were slowly turning into red rose hips. "What is the use of all this beauty if my heart is broken?" she cried.

Weeks passed by and the rosebush felt more and more tired. She was almost into her winter sleep when she heard the voice of her friend who had moved away. She was coming across the road right to her!

"Hello, my beautiful rose. I have missed you so much," said the little grown-up girl.

The wild rose laughed and shook with excitement. Then she realized that the ground around her was also shaking. What was happening? She tried to keep her eyes open to figure it out but she was just too tired.

She drifted into a deep sleep and started to dream. She dreamed her roots and branches were turning into a swallow! She spread her wings and a warm wind lifted her high into a bright blue sky. From there she could see the country mailbox far below and other things she had never seen before. Everything was so clear! There was the little girl's farmhouse with a vegetable garden and flower garden, too. She saw a barn and fields and even a wild rosebush at the edge of a forest. She was going to visit it but then she looked in another direction and saw a puddle on top of a post! Some birds were splashing in it and she decided to join them.

Water sprinkled over her and she blinked her eyes. It was raining but the sun was shining, too. But where was the mailbox? Where were the telephone posts and the wild grasses along the country road?

There was a box but it didn't look like the mailbox she knew because it was on a door. Over it was painted in bright red letters, "HOME IS WHERE THE HEART IS."

Suddenly, the rosebush heard a familiar voice from inside the house. The doorknob turned. The door opened. Out walked her grown-up friend! She bent over the rosebush and touched one of her tender new leaves. A raindrop rolled on to her fingertip.

"Ah! You are awake at last," the grown up little girl whispered softly. "I missed you so much, that I dug you up and brought you to live in the city with me. You have slept right through the winter! I hope you will be happy in your new home."

The wild rosebush laughed in the warm spring breeze and there was a rainbow in the sky. "Home is where the heart is! Home is where the heart is!" the wild rosebush sang over and over again. "Home is where the heart is."

Townsend Place

Years ago we lived on Townsend Place near Queens Park in New Westminster. The area had many old gracious homes, which today are being renovated, as heritage homes. However, when I lived there, most had been converted to multiple suite residences. Because of this, even though there were many single-family homes, realtors called the area "spotty". But such a mixture of inhabitants can have its charm.

The closest such residence was right across our lane. This rectangular structure was so large that it had been turned into five small suites with still enough living space left for the owners. Unfortunately, the landlord was somewhat colour blind. Or maybe he just insisted on only buying paint from the clearance table at the Army and Navy Store on Columbia Street. At any event, he painted the house shrill shades of turquoise, yellow, orange and green and it soon became known as the parrot house.

Sometimes tenants would come across the lane to admire our garden. Occasionally, they would point out the doorway to their particular suite—the owner had added many doors to provide private entrances—and I would bring them a few flowers or apples on occasion.

One woman I befriended was a slim elderly lady called Mabel. Mabel was a superb storyteller and would often talk about books she had read or was reading at the time. She also shared vignettes from her youth such as how she earned pocket money by collecting cascara bark in a local ravine that has long since disappeared. She would dry it, pack it into bags and then tote it down the hill to Buckerfields Store. The ravine has long since been culverted and the store moved to another location. These true life stories touched me the most, as often they were all that remained of a way of life now gone.

Her small suite was decorated with many objects

both crude and elegant. There was, for instance, antique Dresden ink well positioned on the same piece of leather as a railroad spike. Sometimes I would ask about the stories behind such objects and what made them special to her. Mabel would relate such wonderful tales that I promised myself that one day I would ask her to repeat them so I could write them down.

One day, when I had known Mabel for some time, I remarked on the crock that she used to keep the door ajar between the kitchen and her small living room. "Oh", she said softly, looking over at it with a wistful smile, "That is one of the gifts my father gave me." She went over to it, letting the door slowly close as she picked it up and gently touched the lid. "It was always like this," she said, wiping it with her apron and pointing to the chipped lid. "Would you like me to tell you about it?" she asked with a twinkle in her eye.

Even though the crock was very plain—a simpler one could not exist—it became clear that it was very dear to her heart.

I nodded and smiled.

A pale ray of winter sunshine moved across the kitchen floor as memories from her past filled the room. It was such a simple story, with simple ingredients and yet it touched my heart in a strange way.

Later that evening I thought that for once I would write down what I had heard. Of course I couldn't remember it all. Many questions came to mind regarding details she hadn't mentioned. So on subsequent visits the story was flushed out; Mabel was happy that I was writing down "her story".

Finally, I typed it all up—there were no computers in those days—and with just a few words changed, it was complete. I gave it to her to read and, with just a few added particulars. It was complete. Mabel sighed and said it seemed as though it had all happened last week rather than almost fifty years ago.

Noon Hour in the Library

I felt there was something going on which I should know about, but didn't.

"Librarian? Did ya know ya had snakes in the library?"

"What?" I asked, raising my eyebrows. A small group of thirteen-year-old boys, some of the noon hour regulars, assembled around me at the circulation desk.

"Yup. There's twenty-five of 'em. They're crawlin' all over the place."

I looked around.

"Wanna see?" They gleefully pointed to the far wing of the library, an addition which had once been a classroom.

I remained calm (one has to in such situations), but mumbled to myself, "Now what?"

"What're ya goin' to do? What're ya goin' to do now?" they said while elbowing each other with grins on their faces.

Earlier that morning I remembered seeing some boys around a pile of lumber left over from the demolition of the old bus stop. Probably that's where they'd found them.

"I don't know," I answered walking behind them as they led the way. Sure enough, garter snakes were slithering in all directions over the well-worn carpet trying to hide under bookshelves, baseboards and the atlas stand. Some girls were standing on chairs to be safe, others to impress the boys. "We'll need a pail, actually that will do," I said, pointing to an empty tin wastebasket and picking up the closest creature by the tail. One of the boys brought the can over and I dropped it in.

"Aren't ya scared?"

I shrugged. "Why should I be? Sometimes flies

get in the library, sometimes it's reptiles, and you just have to get rid of them. Give me a hand." They nudged each other with their elbows and then with some excited hollering cornered the visitors and dropped them one by one into the metal container.

Finally the boys had rounded up all the garter snakes. They trooped out through the library doors with part of the audience that had gathered around. I heard their footsteps going down the hall. Through the library window I watched them release their captives on the grass next to the pile of lumber at the edge of the school grounds.

For some days there was a lot of talk about my fearlessness. What nobody knew—and I certainly wasn't going to tell them—was that if there had been a bird in the library, just one bird, it would have freaked me out. I have a real phobia about birds.

Put a Gate in Your Garden!

Since ancient times gates have been a symbol of mystery, transition and new beginnings. The month of January is named after the Roman god, Janus, who was the god of doors and gates. An open gate is considered to be the symbol of a shared secret.

Years ago I found an old gate in the creek that runs through our property. It had floated down from who knows where and was lodged between the roots of an old spruce tree and some large rocks. The gate was very narrow, just wide enough for one person to pass through. The top was heart shaped as were the hinges which were still firmly attached. The elements had long ago smoothed and bleached the cedar wood into a soft grey. Since the gate was light I pulled it up the bank and carried it into our garden where it could be admired from several vantage points over the following years.

One spring (I can't remember how long after) I found another old cedar gate lying in an open drainage ditch beside one of the lanes in our area. It also was narrow, but taller than the first, almost shoulder height. This time the hinges were nondescript but the quaint, original latching device was still intact and firmly secured. This gate, which I brought home in the trunk of my car, also added charm to several locations throughout our garden.

Then one day, after I had used these gates as subjects of several garden photographs and water colour paintings, I thought, why not put them into their original use? I placed one gate at the entrance to the herb garden and the other to accent the fact that there was a fork in a pathway. The hinges were rusted tight but that didn't matter because I wanted to keep the doors ajar anyway as welcoming signs in our garden. I simply nailed and/or wired each gate to a post sunk into the ground (actually two old hand split bean poles did the job for one of them) and let variegated ivy grow up to camouflage the hinge area. Pansies in sturdy earthenware pots pretended to be door stops, or should I say gate stops? Since the two gates are permanently open and I am always willing to share gardening "secrets" with friends and neighbours alike, they are very appropriate to our property.

Perhaps you might have an old gate, even a heritage piece, that is looking for a better home. It so happens that bleached cedar looks wonderful in our rustic garden. But materials such as bamboo, metal or twisted branches might suit your individual taste better. Whatever your choice, I am sure you will be pleased with the added dimension a gate makes in your garden.

What's That Sound?

The other morning the weather was cool, or at least not as hot as the previous sun drenched weeks. Clouds were skimming a deep blue sky. An eagle floated on an updraft. A woodpecker was calling. Gentle breezes sighed in the treetops and fluttered the hazelnut bushes— the perfect day for picking blackberries! I slipped into my oldest pair of running shoes, pulled on a long sleeved jacket and rummaged in the cellar to find the pail I had used last year, the one with a piece of binder twine tied to the handle.

I walked down our path and carefully crossed the creek that now because of the dry summer made hardly a sound. Circling past a massive cedar stump still charred from a forest fire that swept down Burnaby Mountain almost a century ago, I climbed up the other side of the ravine finally reaching the fence and turned right.

There were the blackberries already a little warm from the morning sun. Their sweet heavy scent welcomed me. I had checked the spot a few days before. Nobody had discovered the patch. A few berries were already ripe but it had been too hot that morning. Even though early in the day, the sun's heat was already radiating back from the forest's edge. Picking could wait for another day.

Now that day had come. Some blackberry clusters were almost hidden among the deep green and soft burgundy foliage. Others called out for attention. One creeper used a low arching vine maple to reach more sunshine. When I felt that a berry was particularly soft and rolled into my hand with only the gentlest pressure of my thumb, I knew it had to be eaten right away. I popped it into my mouth and savored the mellow sweetness. The rest of the berries made a pleasant drumming noise as they softly thudded into the bottom of the pail.

The sound echoed memories of my childhood in East Chilliwack when I would pick raspberries at the next door neighbours. The wooden tray tied around my waist with binder twine was almost full. I heard something. What was that sound? Probably just a car coming down Prairie Central Road. I lifted up a branch heavy with the weight of raspberries. Bees attacked and stung me all over. Hundreds of them! No wonder that branch was so heavy! I had disturbed a nest of bees! Raspberries bounced out of my tray onto the ground as I ran out of the patch as fast as my skinny legs would take me.

That was a long time ago. My mother used to tell me stories while we were picking raspberries on our farm, straw hats shading our eyes. She told me about her early days in Canada that took place back in 1927 just a few months after she arrived in her mountain shack above the Lower Arrow Lake at Broadwater.

She and my father were returning with buckets of water dipped from the nearby spring. As they turned a bend in the path, two bear cubs were sitting right in front of them, eating blackberries. My father threw a stick to frighten them away. With a loud grunt the mother bear crashed out from the underbrush. The cubs had already scrambled half way up a tree.

"Get the gun!" shouted my father.

Their dog, Trix, raced into the scene and jumped at the massive bear again and again. With zigzag maneuvers he barked and snapped keeping the bear at bay. Yelps pierced the air when the bear's slashing claws met their target. Mother came running with the gun. Dad fired some shots when there was a chance of not hitting the dog. Suddenly the mother bear fled.

Except whimpers from Trix and the comforting sounds of my parent's voices, the wilderness was quiet again.

"It's a true story, not a fairy tale," my mother always said." She disdained fiction and fairy tales. "It came from dealing with real life," she said, "and if it hadn't been for Trix there wouldn't be nothing to tell. Your dad and I would have been dead and you and your sister wouldn't have been born."

Coming back to the present moment, I notice that the old ice cream bucket is almost full. Some rainy day soon there's going to be the aroma of blueberry and blackberry jam coming from the kitchen.

What was that sound? Again that woodpecker's call pierced the morning breeze. I should look. Maybe it's a flicker. They sound about the same, don't they? Where did it go any way? Probably over towards that clearing. I'll look. He's gone.

Now, where did I leave that bucket of blackberries?

The days are shortening. Though the earth still radiates heat from the long days of summer, cool morning breezes caress my face and throat. Golden alder leaves float on a little pond in Stoney Creek. A blue jay alarms the woods. He is searching for hazelnuts. When I walk out of the forest path to a clearing, the aroma of dried grasses and mature seedpods remind me of hop picking days when I played on and under burlap sacks that smelled like dusty sunshine. That was in September, years ago.

As I turn up North Road for my final hike to our house a neighbour drives by giving a cordial wave. He's off to work. It's wonderful having friendly neighbours. One of them calls to me, "Hi, Mother Nature".

Finally back home there's still time to give a drink to the ferns I planted on the other side of the creek. Stoney Creek has never been so low, hardly a murmur, the result of an almost rainless summer. I can only fill the pails half full in the shallow stream, so watering takes a little longer. Give the ferns one more sip.

Damn! Suddenly I'm in the creek, but thank goodness I'm hardly wet and no bones are broken. That's the second time I've slipped and in the very same place! Better be careful. Next time I mightn't be so lucky. Perhaps I should move another rock to make a better step.

It's raining. My gray umbrella blends with the monochromatic world of clouds and pathway. Raindrops tapping overhead like a conductor's baton, sends messages out into nature that it is time to get ready. The stream answers in viola sounds as the scuffing of my shoes on the beaten path provide the hushing rhythm of a tympanum.

On this early February morning there is a lull at forest's edge. Mother Nature seems to be thinking. Winter's cold might soon be over. Nature rests, waiting for the work associated with spring to arrive. There are suggestive swellings on stems, but the rigid hazelnut tassels are still green. The sun's caressing smile has not turned them into golden dancers swaying in the breeze. From deep within the forest I hear only the faintest murmurs as from a stage before a drama is about to begin. A couple of sparrows keep a plaintive vigil among the brambles. But I sense an air of expectancy. Soon the curtains will draw back.

And what will happen in our garden at home? Will the House Finch return again to its home high up in the Norwegian Spruce? Will bushtits do their acrobatic performance in our grapevines and laurel bushes before they continue their migration? Will the tiny Winter Wren hide another nest under our brush-covered bank, its sweet melody singing soprano to the alto of the creek just a few feet below? Will robins build another nest in a fork of our neighbour's magnolia tree? Will the juncos drink from our birdbath? Does the entrance to our new birdhouse face the best direction? Will the nearby bird feeder tempt some chickadees to move in and stay? Time will tell.

Hush! I think I see the curtains moving!

About the Author

Ella Benndorf was born in 1936 of German immigrants on a Fraser Valley homestead near East Chilliwack. When she was two years old her family moved to a large dairy farm at the edge of the West Coast foothills. At the age of thirteen she moved to New Westminster with her mother. After completing high school she married and had a daughter and a son.

In 1970 she and her husband built a home in an old growth forest overlooking Stoney Creek in Oakdale, Coquitlam. She completed her Bachelor of Education at the University of British Columbia and her Master of Education Degree at Simon Fraser University.

After her retirement from her position as a teacher/librarian, she traveled extensively with her husband and became a member of New West Writers. Part of her master's thesis was published in the prestigious German-Canadian Year book as was her illustrated *Logging and Escape from the Wilderness: A Comparison to the Pioneer Life of Susanna Moodie.* She also has been published in both international and national magazines. Her publications include: *For Every Bee There is a Reason* and *Gateways to Shared Secrets.* Her research on North Road, one of British Columbia's oldest roads, as well as other articles, has been published in local community newspapers. She has also written a multicultural cookbook called *Mom's Soup for You.*

In 2001, the author's enthusiasm for the environment and gardening won her several nature garden awards. Her watercolour paintings often reflect the wilderness and vestiges of pioneer life. She named two creeks in Oakdale: *Harmony* and *Consultation,* and was a founding member of Salmonoid Enhancement Program in Coquitlam. Her nomination for the YWCA Women of Distinction was due mainly to work in her community of Oakdale and multiculturalism.

She became a Baha'i in 1969 and since then has been very active in working for the oneness of mankind.

The author's discovery of her father's letters dating from the middle of World War I until her mother left Bavaria for Canada in 1927 proved to be the catalyst for research into the social history of those times. Her parents met at a beekeeping course where a priest pointed out Aloisia as being a very suitable prospect for marriage. Though initially reluctant, she was finally persuaded to correspond with him. He wrote letters from his ship even when it was anchored at Scapa Flow. He wrote from his family farm, from Argentina and finally from the prairies and wilderness of the Canadian Rockies. To Aloisia's shock, an isolated hunting shack virtually hanging from a mountainside became her new home. *Aloisia, The Making of a*

Pioneer Woman reveals gripping dilemmas including the universal challenges intrinsic to human nature: love, betrayal, hope, and those qualities every settler to the New World requires in full measure—courage and determination.

Made in the USA
Columbia, SC
27 July 2018